THE SEEKER'S GUIDE TO

Reading the Bible

Thanks for sharing
this Bible journey!
Steve Mueller

Other books in the Seeker Series include

Living the Beatitudes Today
Bill Dodds and Michael J. Dodds, O.P.

The Seeker's Guide to Being Catholic
Mitch Finley

The Seeker's Guide to 7 Life-Changing Virtues
Bill Dodds and Michael J. Dodds, O.P.

The Seeker's Guide to the Christian Story
Mitch Finley

Chicago

THE SEEKER'S GUIDE TO

Reading
the Bible

a Catholic View

 Loyola Press

Chicago

STEVE MUELLER

 Loyola Press

3441 North Ashland Avenue
Chicago, Illinois 60657

The Seeker Series *from Loyola Press provides trustworthy guides for your journey of faith and is dedicated to the principle that asking questions is not only all right . . . it is essential.*

Cover and interior design by Lisa Buckley
Cover image courtesy of Tony Stone Images

Library of Congress Cataloging-in-Publication Data
Mueller, Steve.
    The seeker's guide to reading the Bible / Steve Mueller.
        p. cm. — (Seeker series)
    ISBN 0-8294-1345-6 (pbk.)
    1. Bible Introductions. 2. Catholic Church — Doctrines.
  I. Title. II. Series: Seeker series (Chicago, Ill.)
  BS475.2.M84 1999
  220.6 — dc21   99-28198
                                             CIP

Printed in the United States of America
99 00 01 02 03 / 10 9 8 7 6 5 4 3 2 1

Contents

A Word to the Seeker

I crave the reader's indulgence
over the explanation of a text
whose obscurity is due to three causes:
the difficulty of the text itself,
the incompetence of the master
and the inexperience of the disciple.

—*ST. JEROME*
Commentary on Hosea

Thirty years of teaching and many more of learning have taught me the essential truth that every seeker must learn sooner or later: Although there are plenty of dumb answers, there is no such thing as a dumb question! Since I do not know exactly what your questions might be, my *Seeker's Guide to Reading the Bible* will address many of the problems and concerns that adult learners commonly face when they begin to read and study the Bible.

Who needs a book like this? People who want to learn how to see beyond the surface of their ordinary lives into a mysterious world charged with God's presence and activity. Reading your Bible is a fantastic adventure on which you will experience and explore the fascinating and surprising world of the Bible.

If you want to take up your Bible and travel its pathways, this book will both inform you about the Bible and acquaint you with the skills needed to read and heed its message. Like any good guidebook, this seeker's guide will help you prepare for your journey and make it more enjoyable.

Part One, Deciding to Make Your Journey, encourages you to choose this special biblical trip from among the many possible ways you can spend your time. As you progress through this section, you will learn how to overcome your fears, why your Bible is different from other books, and how to approach reading and interpreting the Bible from a Catholic perspective.

Part two, Preparing for Your Journey, helps you get ready for the trip by offering a quick tour through the Bible. This overview explains how the Bible is organized and gives a brief history of the composition and collection of its books. This part of the book also investigates the connection between the biblical authors and their audiences and provides lists of possible reference materials to equip you for your journey.

Part three, Making Your Journey, first suggests a practical itinerary for your initial reading journey. This list ensures that you will read every book of the Bible. Then I offer practical helps so that you'll be encouraged to pick up your Bible and read it. I suggest an effective reading method that is "as easy as ABC." I then describe how you can get help from Scripture scholars to deal with some problems that arise when we read the Bible. Finally, since sharing your journey always makes the trip more enjoyable, I suggest a way that you can bring God's Word to life through group discussion. At the end of most chapters there are also suggested questions for reflection and group discussion. The glossary contains some important biblical terms that every seeker should recognize.

I would like to thank the many seekers who have shared my Bible journey and have discovered the God who lies hidden beyond the living words of the text. In particular, I especially enjoyed my journey with the faculty and staff of the Denver Catholic Biblical School — Sr. Macrina Scott, Angeline Hubert, Sr. Dorothy Jonaitis, Kathy McGovern, and Helen Williams — and with the many hundreds of students and graduates who over the years taught me so much about Bible country and the God of surprises who dwells there.

I wish to offer very special thanks to my wife, Mary, and our four children — Drew, Johanna, Luke, and Margaret — for the love and support they have so abundantly given me on our family journey together.

Finally, to all of you seekers, I hope this book opens up new vistas for you. Enjoy your journey. I wish you well. As I finish this writing, I feel like the ancient biblical scholar St. Jerome, who once observed:

"I am not stupid enough to feel hurt if you put forward explanations different from mine. Neither should you feel hurt if my opinion contradicts yours. I have had my time, and I have run as far as I could. Now it is time for you to run — for you to cover the long tracks. It is time for me to rest" *(LETTER 102).*

PART ONE

Deciding to Make Your Journey

What is sacred Scripture but a kind of letter from Almighty God to us creatures? And surely, if you were resident somewhere else, and were to receive letters from an earthly emperor, you would not loiter, you would not rest, you would not sleep until you had learned what the emperor had written. . . . Study then and daily meditate on the words of your creator. Learn the heart of God in the words of God, so that you may desire more ardently the things that are eternal, that your soul may be kindled with greater longings for heavenly joys. . . . May God pour into you the Spirit, the Comforter. May you be filled with God's presence, and in being filled, be composed.

POPE GREGORY I (THE GREAT)
Letter to Theodorus, Physician to the Emperor (ca. A.D 595)

CHAPTER ONE

The Journey That Will Change Your Life

Let's face it. For most of us Catholics, the Bible is like a foreign country. We have heard fascinating stories about its people and places from others who have traveled there. We might even have met someone who, like some spiritual secret agent, has been a closet Bible reader for years without ever revealing these undisclosed excursions into Bible country. Although most of us might have secretly yearned to make this journey, for various reasons we have never done it ourselves.

For years, most Catholics recorded births, baptisms, first communions, and weddings in their family Bible but never dreamed of reading it. They had been warned that there were too many dangers in traveling there on their own. "Private interpretation" was especially suspect and dangerous because it could lead directly to heresy.

Despite this, when their curiosity got the best of them, many Catholics decided to read the Bible. Since our modern Bible is bound like a book, they assumed that they should read it from cover to cover, only to find it obscure, puzzling, and even boring. Like so many other confused and discouraged seekers, they usually quit after the first few books.

But the Bible has retained its fascination for us. We are like the great seeker St. Augustine some sixteen hundred years ago, who tells of his conversion experience in his autobiographical *Confessions* (bk 8.12). Disillusioned by his superficial lifestyle and reluctant to enter into a deeper relationship with God, he heard a child who was playing chant, "Take and read, take and read."

"Sacred Scripture changes the heart of whoever reads it from earthly desires to embracing spiritual things. . . . In some way it grows with the persons reading, so that for uninstructed readers it is a review, and for well-instructed readers it is always new. . . . Sacred Scripture by the manner of its speech transcends every science, because in one and the same sentence, while it describes a fact, it reveals a mystery."

— *POPE GREGORY I (THE GREAT)*
Morals on the Book of Job, Book XX (ca. A.D. 585)

Assuming that this meant his Bible, Augustine opened it randomly to a passage from St. Paul's letter to the Romans (13:13 – 14), which urged him to cast aside the past and begin a new relationship with God. As seekers, our intuition tells us that something good will happen when we heed the faint voices we hear prompting us to "take and read" our Bible.

Tourist or Resident?

If the Bible is like a foreign country, then reading the Bible is how we journey there. Just as there are many travel guides and videos to acquaint us with places we would like to visit, there are many helpful introductory books and study programs that help us understand more about the Bible. But watching a *National Geographic* video from the comfort of our living room is never like being there in person. Likewise, no amount of secondhand knowledge about the Bible can substitute for the firsthand experience of reading it.

The journey to Bible country must ultimately be made in person because what we are seeking is not simply bits of information or good ideas about God. The Bible is not an "infomercial," selling God like some product we can acquire. It is a guidebook for our relationship with God.

Bible reading is different from most other reading that we do. Reading the Bible demands that we take more time to pause and examine our familiar world. Only when we do this can we discover the mysterious divine realities that normally go unnoticed. Reading the Bible from cover to cover to get a quick overview of its contents is like taking the whirlwind tour of Europe that provides merely a surface awareness. If it's Tuesday, this must be Paris!

How different it would be to live in Paris for weeks or months and absorb the experience of being there with Parisians! When we journey into Bible country, we do not want to be just tourists. We want to be sojourners — foreigners who enjoy the new region so much that they take up residence and perhaps even become citizens.

The Bible journey is a unique trip. It is not exactly a business trip, although we will profit from the journey. It is not exactly a vacation, although we will be refreshed and recharged if we go. The Bible journey is unique because it takes us to the center of our faith to meet this mysterious other called God. It is not an outward journey that traverses the geography of the land but an inner journey over the landscape of our relationship with God.

Through our biblical journey, we have the opportunity to refresh our vision of what our world is like, rethink our values, and change our behavior because of our relationship with God. Our desire is not just for theology — faith seeking understanding — but for spirituality — faith seeking embodiment. The Bible is the doorway that leads us from our ordinary, material, external world to a spiritual, extraordinary, inner one. God stands at the door and invites, but we have to decide to step across the threshold.

The Bible Journey: Taking Care of Sacred Business

Whether we recognize it or not, our journey into Bible territory always begins with some agenda. Why do we want to read the Bible and not some other book? There are thousands of books about religion, prayer, spirituality, psychology, history, and so on. Why not read one of those? Answering this question for yourself is the first step on the journey.

The main business we are all in is that of self-making. Our lifetime is a journey, and this journey shapes and defines us. Self-making occurs also as we relate to others; these relationships help us discover who we are and what our gifts are. Ultimately, we find our identity in relationship to God, the divine other who calls us into a special relationship. The Bible is our primary resource for discovering God's plan for who we are to become.

Like the business and economic activity that dominate so much of our everyday lives, our personal or sacred "business" also requires much time and effort. Just as a business trip has definite goals in mind, our trip through the Bible ought to have some bottom-line payoff for us. As the American philosopher William James liked to say, religious ideas also need some "cash value." What is the practical application or usefulness of our Bible journey for our business of self-making?

Bible reading can deepen our spiritual life.

Since reading the Bible opens up the often neglected spiritual depths of our world and ourselves, it can jump-start our personal spiritual life and help us live out our relationship to God much more consciously.

As we notice how and where God is present, we become more spiritually aware and see our familiar world through the eyes of faith. Reading the Bible reveals that the surface appearances of our self and our everyday world hide a deeper mystery that normally escapes our notice.

WHAT ARE YOU LOOKING FOR?
Five Concerns That Focus Our Approaches to the Bible

Basic Beliefs (theology)

Information (history)

Being Together (community, tradition, worship)

Life Guidelines (both moral and practical)

Expressions of Our Relationship to God (prayer)

Just as the disciples discovered Jesus alive after his death, so each of us as Christians has also experienced the living presence of Jesus. This living presence lures us onward into the mystery of the God who surrounds and supports us and desires to relate to us. We recognize God's presence in the various experiences and events that hint at life beyond our everyday material realities. There is always more than meets the eye! And this "more" is God.

The Bible is our primary handbook for learning how to live in a religious relationship with God. As seekers, we want to discover God's presence and then learn how to be in effective contact with God. The word *religion* comes from the Latin word meaning to "retie" something. Religion encompasses our efforts to retie ourselves to God in the kind of relationship that God wishes.

Although we often equate faith with accepting a list of doctrines, faith is essentially our commitment to God and our relationship with God. The root of the word *faith* in Latin means the "bond" that establishes and sustains a relationship. This is synonymous with our sense of trust. When we trust someone, we entrust ourselves to him or her. Our care and commitment to others in relationships always involves greater sharing. Our Bible reading recalls for us the long history of other seekers who have discovered God and committed themselves to a more conscious relationship. We can learn from their example.

Bible reading can help us change our priorities.

As we begin to live a more conscious spiritual life, the effects ripple out to every part of our life. By encouraging us to look seriously at our relationships with God and with one another, Bible reading changes our priorities. By learning to notice

God's presence and activity, we add a spiritual component — we include God! And changing our priorities will affect how we make decisions about how to live. Making decisions does not necessarily become easier, but we see more clearly what is at stake and become more aware of what values guide us.

Bible reading can help us deepen our family life.

Changing our priorities through Bible reading helps us to deepen our family life because it constantly draws our attention to the task of living out our significant relationships. The Bible is a handbook for right relationships. It shows us where some other seekers have found God, how they were changed by that encounter, and how they found others with whom they could live in right relationship to God.

God calls us into relationships and makes demands about how we ought to live. Every relationship demands creating a community — a co-mission with the other. When lovers commit themselves to one another, their co-mission is to build a family. When believers join together, their co-mission is to create God's dream community. The Bible provides help for understanding our common goal and the cost it will take to achieve it.

Bible reading can help us reorient our work life.

If we can begin to see our work as a vocation rather than just a job, then the meaning of our work changes. Since meaning comes when we connect what we are doing to something else, the meaning of our work changes when we connect it to our relationship with God and our co-mmission to create the kind of relationships with others that God desires.

Bible reading can help us find more meaning in life.
Meaning cannot occur in isolation. Words become meaningful when we connect them together into sentences and arrange them into ever larger paragraphs and chapters. Meaning comes through placing elements into contexts.

So the meaning of our life as a whole comes when we put all the pieces together and then relate it to some larger context. For some this might be their family, for others a corporation or project. For religious persons the wider context is God's reality. The Bible provides the context in which our lives can be understood. We are called to be in relationship with God in a community of fellow believers. Reading the Bible brings us face-to-face with God, who wants to be in relationship with us. Relationships take time and effort. Our Bible journey is a lifetime journey with this divine companion. It offers a way for us to stop, take time with God, and revitalize our relationship.

Discovering New Worlds

One of the best things about going on a trip is that we visit new places and see new sights. The reading journey involves movement both into and through a new world, along with reflection about the significance of what we are seeing. As we travel in this new world, we need to discuss what is happening to us.

"Indeed the authority of Scripture seemed more to be revered and more worthy of devoted faith in that it was at once a book that all could read and read easily, and yet preserved the majesty of its mystery in the deepest part of its meaning: for it offers itself to all in the plainest words and the simplest expressions, yet demands the closest attention of the most serious minds."

— *ST. AUGUSTINE*
Confessions, 6:5

Travel always helps us see our culture and ourselves in a new way because we step out of our ordinary perspective. Seeing the world through the eyes of a different culture lets us notice more clearly our own culture.

Whether our ordinary life includes God in it or not, by traveling to Bible country we have the opportunity to adopt the perspective that puts God at the center of the world. In the biblical world, God's presence is the central organizing factor around which everything revolves. Through our reading, we are invited to reorient our ordinary lives along the coordinates of meaning and purpose that we have discovered in the biblical world.

The biblical standpoint and perspective produce a "culture shock" that challenges our understanding of the way things ought to be and our priorities for everyday living. This demands changes in our behavior if we are going to live according to our new understanding. Reading the Bible keeps alive the dangerous notion that there is a hidden reality beyond the world of appearances. And that reality is God!

Meeting New and Fascinating People

Another great advantage of traveling is meeting new and fascinating people. The Bible is full of seekers like us. Each character helps us with our search to discover God's presence and to respond to it. Journeying into Bible country brings us face-to-face with a whole array of strange and mysterious people.

Meeting new people is always risky. We never know what effect they will have on us. This confrontation with another can confirm and comfort us, confront and challenge us, or surprise and renew us. Journeying to Bible country can confirm our cherished beliefs and behaviors or challenge us to adopt a fresh vision and different values because of the people we discover along the way.

Meeting new people always puts us on the alert for new ways of communicating and relating to others. Each biblical character shows us unique responses to God's presence, which express his or her relationship to God. Communities also take on distinctive traits as they embody God's dream for the right kind of community.

THE JOURNEY THAT WILL CHANGE YOUR LIFE

Of course the most fascinating personality of all is God. The Bible portrays God in all the mysterious diversity of a real person. God is the main character throughout the biblical story. Through God's actions and words we discover who God is and how God likes to relate to us. The Bible preserves the memory of God's relationship to us.

"The scholar, the student of the Bible, is first of all an ardent and fearless listener to the divine message. He knows that it is not a dead letter locked away in archival documents, but rather a living and still intact message that comes from God and is to be welcomed in its entirety with the open, and we might say the impassioned, mind with which it was listened to by the prophets, the apostles, and the countless legions of people who feared God in the Old and the New Testament."

POPE JOHN XXIII
Address to the Italian Biblical Association (24 September 1962)

Through reading the Bible we become familiar with God's personality and what God expects from us. The main story of the Bible is God's desire to have a people who exemplify the way to live. First with the Israelites, and then with Christians, God seeks a community that is the sign and model of God's loving presence among us.

For us Christians, meeting Jesus through the Gospels is usually a new experience. Whatever we might know about Jesus comes alive as we hear his words and consider his actions. We discover his agenda for the right relationship with God and with one another. No one can encounter Jesus through the Gospels and remain untouched by this experience. One author describes reading the Bible as an adult as meeting Jesus again for the first time! Jesus never loses his fascination and mystery as God's revelation in human form.

Experiencing the Bible through reading brings us out of our comfort zone into a strange and unfamiliar world. No matter how much we think we already know about the God of the Bible or about Jesus, we are constantly surprised when we begin to meet them anew in the pages of the Bible.

What Are You Seeking?

We are mistaken, though, to think that God will be found in the pages of the book. The Bible does not give us God. Rather, it shows us where God has been found by some other seekers, how they were changed by that encounter, and how they attempted to find ways to live with others in relationship to the God they had discovered.

We learn what the Bible means as we relate it to our life. Like any book, the story, characters, and themes take on increased significance when we decide that they mean more than what we find between the covers of the book. When we connect what we read with something in our life, then we'll remember what we read, and we'll let it shape us. For this reason, our Bible reading journey does not just inform but transforms. As we move beyond simply amassing scraps of information to being shaped by the meanings we discover.

The journey of Bible reading, like every journey, is full of surprises. It is a mixture of anticipation and anxiety, fun and fear. The unknown stirs up anxieties in all of us. We do not know what will face us and whether or not we will be able to handle what does come. But often our curiosity gets the better of us, and we venture out to experience something new that we know will change our lives.

Questions for Reflection and Group Discussion

1. *What is going on in your life that points you toward the Bible and not some other book?*
2. *Is reading the Bible more like business or pleasure for you? Why?*
3. *How would you rank the following goals for Bible reading:*
   ____ basic beliefs,
   ____ historical information,
   ____ community life and worship,
   ____ moral guidelines for living,
   ____ prayer? Share the reasons for your rankings.
4. *Have you ever been to a foreign country? Share two things that were very different there — one that you liked and another that you disliked.*

THE TOP TEN REASONS FOR READING YOUR BIBLE

10. You will never have to worry about choosing the Bible category on *Jeopardy.*

9. You can get a jump start for your spiritual life.

8. You can watch late-night cable TV and not worry about the end of the world.

7. You can travel to the heart of God without leaving your living room.

6. You won't hesitate to talk to strangers about the apocalypse.

5. You'll learn how to avoid the dumb mistakes smart people make in relating to God.

4. You'll be able to explain why B-I-B-L-E means "Basic Instructions Before Leaving Earth."

3. You will discover secrets about the quirky religious family you belong to.

2. You can meet Jesus again for the first time.

1. You will come face-to-face with the God who loves you.

CHAPTER TWO

Overcoming Your Fear of Bible Travel

Reading the Bible is a dangerous venture. When we go beyond our usual boundaries, we never quite know what will happen. The further we travel from our home, where everything is familiar and our comfort level is high, the more likely we are to meet people who are unlike us.

Journeys change us because they take us across the boundaries that keep us comfortably insulated from worlds that are different from ours. Whenever we go to a new place and meet new people, we risk change. Just as we risk the possibility of change whenever we venture out of our neighborhood — or our country — so we will be vulnerable if we venture outside our familiar religious worldview. In all my years of teaching the Bible to adults, the one constant certainty was this: As we work on God's Word, God's Word works on us.

Four Common Fears and How to Overcome Them

Deciding to embark on the journey of Bible reading is not always easy. We have doubts, anxieties, and fears about this trip, just as we would about any physical journey. *What if I don't know enough about the land or the people or the language? What if the journey is more hazardous than I imagined? What if I encounter situations that will demand that I change? What if I get lost and cannot find my way back?*

Fear of the unfamiliar can paralyze us and keep us from making the journey that we know will change us. For most Bible seekers, there are four fears that, more than anything else, prevent us from making the biblical journey: fear of ignorance, fear of inadequacy, fear of change, and fear of getting lost.

If we are to overcome these fears, we must increase our trust. In Bible country, the opposite of fear is faith. Faith emphasizes trust in God rather than merely an intellectual acceptance of doctrines. Jesus, for example, tells a father seeking help for his dying daughter, "Do not fear; only believe" (Mark 5:36).

We, too, must heed this invitation of Jesus. These fears that threaten to keep us from our journey can be overcome if we notch up our trust — trust in the one who calls us, in ourselves as seekers, and in our companions who walk with us.

Fear 1: I'm too dumb

The most common fear when approaching the formidable journey of Bible reading is that we are not smart enough. We have been told either directly or indirectly that the Bible is so complicated that we must leave its interpretation to the experts. And since they are always disagreeing, what hope can there be for an ordinary layperson to understand it?

Well, trust yourself as a reader. The Bible was not written for scholars but for ordinary people who were far less educated than you are! Since most of the original readers could not read at all, the Bible was read out loud to them. They had no extra helps or commentaries except the guidance of someone in the community who had a little more knowledge than they did.

> "It is no small gain
> to know your own ignorance."
> — *ST. JEROME*
> Letter 61

The biblical journey is not a head trip. The message of the Bible is not some complicated abstract doctrine. If that were the case, then the authors would probably have chosen to write it as philosophical essays. The Bible is a collection of the treasured memories of a family relationship. It is meant to change your life, not just your ideas.

Trust yourself to discover the message about God and God's purpose that is there for you. Be humble enough to recognize that what you discover need not match exactly what others are looking for. Dialogue with others is always essential to focus on the truths that are hidden in God's Word. Holding the Bible in our hands is a lot easier than holding its message in our hearts. This assimilation takes a lifetime of conversion.

Many adult Catholics also carry a subtle sense of shame along with this feeling of ignorance. We feel that we ought to already know more about the Bible. We assume that everybody else knows so much more than we do. Even our kids seem more Bible literate than we are! We hide our ignorance lest others discover that we are biblical illiterates.

First of all, accept the fact that you do not know much. Being "biblically challenged" is nothing to be ashamed of! Knowing that you *don't* know is where all seekers begin. Like the Greek philosopher Socrates, who was identified as the wisest man in Athens because he admitted that there was so much he did not know, acknowledge your ignorance, and increase your desire to learn. This is what seeking is all about.

Second, keep in mind that you don't have to become an expert on the Bible, but you do need to become a more competent reader. (Really, there are few areas of life in which you are expected to be an expert!) Becoming a more serious reader who can read the Bible carefully and with ever increasing sensitivity is the goal to strive for. The more you know about the Bible and how to read it, the better you will understand God's message.

Fear 2: It's too hard

We have been told that reading the Bible is dangerous and that people read it incorrectly. We hear endless debates on late-night TV about what the Bible really means. We tend to think, *Since it takes scholars so many years to acquire competence to read it, it is certainly too complicated for a regular person like me to understand. Just leave it to the experts who really know what they are doing.*

"Exegetes may have a distinctive role in the interpretation of the Bible but they do not exercise a monopoly. This activity within the Church has aspects which go beyond the academic analysis of texts. The Church, indeed, does not regard the Bible simply as a collection of historical documents dealing with its own origins; it receives the Bible as the word of God, addressed both to itself and to the entire world at the present time."

— PONTIFICAL BIBLICAL COMMISSION
The Interpretation of the Bible in the Church (1993)

Again, trust your own ability as a reader. I am often reminded of the biblical story of David and Goliath. Goliath was a giant whose size struck fear in everyone. When David

OVERCOMING YOUR FEAR OF BIBLE TRAVEL

offered to meet Goliath in combat, the soldiers assumed that David could fight only if he donned the armor of King Saul. Since the king's armor was not David's size, it was far too unwieldy to help. So David reverted to his own tried-and-true sling and five smooth stones.

We do not have to read the Bible using the elaborate methods of Scripture scholarship. The scholars' sophisticated methods are very important, and their conclusions yield meanings that would often remain unnoticed. But these methods are always refinements of the basic questions that curious and careful readers will ask about any text.

Books are written to be read. Biblical books were written to reveal something to us about God and about our relationship with God. Our most basic rule for reading is simply to know what we are doing and why we are doing it. As long as we are careful in our reading and understand the potential pitfalls, we can usually read the Bible with much profit. As always, we must remember that the goal of our reading is not scholarly information but the transformation of ourselves in our relationship with God.

We can also use the helps available for better reading. There are many books that give a sense of the times in which the biblical books were written and the messages they conveyed to their original audiences. Entrust yourself to guides who are competent and know their way. They will not let you go astray.

Fear 3: It's too threatening

Seekers know that venturing into unfamiliar territory will change them. Holding the Bible in our hands can be comforting. Hearing and heeding its message in our hearts is much more difficult. Reading the Bible is an invitation to a relationship that will bring us into regions we usually dare not enter. So we have that sneaking feeling that what we find in the Bible will not always be comfortable for us.

Bible reading invites us to encounter a divinely charged reality that always involves more than we can imagine or comfortably manage in our present experience. Touching the divine transforms us forever. Can we let ourselves be drawn in directions we would never choose and be transformed by our journey? There is no way to meet God and ever be the same again.

As the Jewish prophet Jeremiah warned so long ago, we dare to make the journey to meet God only because we have been called by God into this relationship, or "how else should one take the deadly risk of approaching me? says the LORD" (Jeremiah 30:21, NAB) But it is a "deadly risk" we must take if we want to live in relationship with God.

This is the risk we all face when we say yes to God. Living in relationship to God is always a challenge. When we decide to live more responsibly in the light of our commitment to this relationship, the obligations of that relationship will require some changes in us. We must accept the risk of living fully in relation to God. God is satisfied with nothing less than the sacrifice — the making holy — of our whole self. We must be both holy and whole.

This relationship stamps our lives. But it is a "deadly risk" because we will have to change our perceptions of who we are, what we think, and how we act. These do not change easily, because they have become part of us as we have grown up in our family, our society, and our Church. Physically, we begin to die from the moment we are born. Spiritually, we begin to die to an old way of being from the moment we make our faith commitment to be in relationship with God and to live more responsibly.

We overcome this fear of personal change only as we entrust ourselves to God. We can trust that the changes that follow will be good ones because they are what God desires. We must be willing to die to ourselves — our ego, our old vision of reality, our old values, and our old behaviors — in order to be transformed. To see the world the way Jesus does, to value it as Jesus does, and to act in it as Jesus does will lead us into a new relationship with God. We will be transformed in a way that will no longer entail the "deadly risk" that haunts us now.

Fear 4: I might get lost

Anyone who has tried to read the Bible on their own has had this fear overtake them just about the time they get to the books of Leviticus and Numbers. After reading the exciting stories in the books of Genesis and Exodus — about the patriarch Abraham and his family, the escapades that landed them in Egypt, their oppression, and finally their exhilarating exodus under the leadership of Moses — we suddenly feel as stranded in the wilderness as the wandering Hebrews were.

Usually, at this point we put down the Bible and assume that there is nothing there for us. We mistakenly believe that if we try to travel into this territory again, we may never come out alive. We return to our everyday lives without ever discovering the Bible's hidden treasures or how to apply them to our lives.

In order to overcome this fear, we have to realize that making the biblical journey might best be done under the guidance of one we can trust. Like the American settlers who decided to brave the trip across the prairies to a new life, we need to entrust our journey to a scout who knows the trails because he or she has been there before. The scout is able not only to show the way but also to warn us of potential dangers. If we choose our guides well, we can trust them to lead us to the destination we seek.

We must also remember that we never read the Bible alone. All reading assumes a community that shares the language and the conventions of reading. Without this community, interpretation is impossible. The community in which the interpretation of the Bible occurs is the Christian Church.

The Bible belongs to the Church before it belongs to any individual.

Reading for meaning always requires that we test our conclusions against those of other readers. We read the Bible in the whole tradition of believers for whom this book has been the privileged guide to life in relationship with God. Not only scholars but also the official teaching office of the Church have always been concerned with right reading. If we entrust ourselves to the guidelines of the Church for reading the Scriptures, then we can know that we will not go wrong.

Our Bible journey can also be more fun if we encourage other seekers to accompany us. Just as traveling invites comments about what we have seen and done, so Bible reading invites comments about what we are experiencing and how it is affecting us. Companions on the journey make travel much more interesting and enjoyable. Talking with others also provides a good sounding board for testing our impressions and conclusions.

Traveler's Tips for Making the Bible Journey

Bible reading, and the relationship with God that it nourishes, can be the most fascinating, the most rewarding, and sometimes the most frustrating journey you will ever take. Seasoned travelers who have made the journey can offer advice that helps us. They know what we ought to carry with us and what we should abandon as useless. Here are four traveler's tips that are particularly helpful.

Tip 1: Don't worry about the Bible; worry about yourself

Often we get defensive about God and the Bible — especially when relating to those skeptics who question our religious claims more than we do. When embarking on the Bible journey, it is best not to worry so much about the Bible as about yourself. The Bible has weathered all the storms of more than two thousand years of aggressive and critical scrutiny.

The Bible was written to be read, and it can be read for many different reasons and in a variety of contexts. We can never assume that we have exhausted the divinely revealed mysteries contained in it. New questions about the text are always being discovered. It will take the lifetime of the Church to understand the Bible.

We need to worry more about ourselves as readers. Making the message of the Bible our own and applying it to our lives require effort. Are we willing to take time with the Bible, to learn what it says and consider seriously what it means, and to use our knowledge to live a better Christian life?

Tip 2: Don't try to control the Bible

The Bible is a tool for living. Like any tool, it can't volunteer to be used. We have to decide to use it to accomplish our goals. Our skill determines how effective we are. But although the user is normally in charge of a tool, the reader does not control God's Word. We will be mistaken if we assume that, like ordinary tools, the Bible is strictly under our control.

The Bible can be used for a variety of tasks. Learning to use the Bible in our lives demands the skills of reading, interpretation, and application. Moreover, as our lives change, we will need to use these skills to apply the Bible to our relationship to God and to other people.

God controls the Bible's utterance as well as its meaning. We have no control over the minds and speech of other people, and we have no control over God's Word. What the text reveals is not up to us but up to God. We can spend a lifetime trying to control God, but it never works. The Bible reminds us over and over that despite our most strenuous efforts, we can never manipulate God. God's ways are not always our ways, and we cannot force God into our molds. This hard lesson forces us always to let God be God.

Just as it is a waste of energy to use the wrong tool, so it is unwise to use the Bible to pressure others to do what we think they ought to do. By all means, share what you are learning with your family, your friends and coworkers, and other seekers you encounter along the way. But you do not have to use the Bible as if it were a hammer to beat them into submission or convert them to your ways of thinking and of doing things.

"Sacred tradition and Sacred Scripture form one sacred deposit of the word of God, committed to the Church. Holding fast to this deposit the entire holy people united with their shepherds remain always steadfast in the teaching of the apostles, in the common life, in the breaking of the bread and in prayers, so that holding to, practicing and professing the heritage of the faith, it becomes on the part of the bishops and faithful a single common effort.

"But the task of authentically interpreting the word of God, whether written or handed on, has been entrusted exclusively to the living teaching office of the Church, whose authority is exercised in the name of Jesus Christ. This teaching office is not above the word of God, but serves it, teaching only what has been handed on, listening to it devoutly, guarding it scrupulously and explaining it faithfully in accord with a divine commission and with the help of the Holy Spirit, it draws from this one deposit of faith everything which it presents for belief as divinely revealed.

"It is clear, therefore, that sacred tradition, Sacred Scripture and the teaching authority of the Church, in accord with God's most wise design, are so linked and joined together that one cannot stand without the others, and that all together and each in its own way under the action of the one Holy Spirit contribute effectively to the salvation of souls."

— *VATICAN COUNCIL II*
Dogmatic Constitution on Divine Revelation, #10

Acknowledge that although the paths that others follow might be different from yours, those paths might also lead to God, who can be found in surprising places. Take a lesson from the master Jesus, who, in a gentle and kindly way, imparts the message of God's presence in our midst and of God's rule over our world. This respect for others and an appreciation of their personal discovery of God will encourage them to take the unique journey to which God is calling them.

Tip 3: Get ready for surprises

The Bible journey is full of surprises. When people share with one another what they are discovering, it becomes clear that the Bible is full of endless meanings and applications. One reason for this is that the divinely revealed realities about God can never be fully fathomed by our human minds. *The truth of the Bible is not the truth of a proposition but the truth of a person.* The Bible text illuminates us, guides us, and helps us. But it also challenges us and calls into question who we are and how we live.

Another reason is that meanings change when contexts do. When our reading situation and our personal needs change, our discoveries in the Bible will change too. I am astounded when I look at my dog-eared student Bible and see how in my eager enthusiasm I triple underlined a passage and wrote "Wow — this says it all!!!" in the margin. Looking at that today, I have no idea why that passage was so significant then — and is so insignificant today.

As you make your Bible journey, then, know that whatever you think you know about God and about Christ is never the full answer. Being in a relationship with someone else is a never ending surprise about both the other and you. Live the Bible's questions and let them challenge you. When what you read makes you uncomfortable, you can be sure that this is a sign from God about where you need to grow.

Tip 4: Enjoy your journey

Bible reading helps us discover that God is present in our lives and eager to enter a relationship with us. God has called us on the journey so that we can live a fuller and more spiritual life. Although following this spiritual path can make us anxious, it is essential if we are to meet the Lord. The Old Testament patriarch Jacob, Abraham's grandson whose name was later changed to Israel, had a famous dream about a staircase leading up to heaven. The Bible is a sort of staircase for us, allowing us to approach God and God to draw near to us. Upon waking, Jacob realized that "the LORD is in this spot, although I did not know it!" (Genesis 28:16, NAB).

So as we begin this journey, let us pray as Jacob did:

If God remains with me, to protect me on this journey I am making and to give me enough bread to eat and clothing to wear, and I come back safe to my father's house, the LORD shall be my God. (Genesis 28:20–21)

"The truth cannot impose itself except by virtue of its own truth, as it makes its entrance into the mind at once quietly and with power. . . . Truth is to be sought after in a manner proper to the dignity and social nature of the human person. The inquiry is to be free, carried on with the aid of teaching or instruction, communication, and dialogue. In the course of these, people explain to one another the truth they have discovered, or think they have discovered, in order thus to assist one another in the quest for truth. Moreover, as the truth is discovered, it is by a personal assent that people are to adhere to it."

— *VATICAN COUNCIL II*
Declaration on Religious Freedom, #1, 3

Questions for Reflection and Group Discussion

1. *Which of the four common fears of Bible reading most paralyzes you? Why?*
2. *What other fears do you have concerning your Bible reading journey?*
3. *What do you expect to find out about God from the Bible?*
4. *What advice about God do you like to quote to others?*

CHAPTER THREE

Why Your Bible Is Different from Other Books

For Catholic Christians, the Bible is not just another book on the local bookstore shelf. We have certain beliefs about the Bible before we ever come to read it. In brief, as Vatican Council II expressed it, we believe that our Bible is "the words of God, expressed in human language" *(Dogmatic Constitution on Divine Revelation,* November 18, 1965, no. 13). Our Bible is not just a book; it's our sacred book.

As sacred, our Bible is the book we pick up when we want to know about God and our relationship with God. Reading the Bible provides clues about the reality of God and cues for responding to God in appropriate ways. The biblical story is the story of God with us, and this story continues to shape our lives.

Our goal here is not to argue in detail about our Catholic beliefs about the Bible but rather to acknowledge them and understand how they influence our approach to the Bible. These assumptions do not come explicitly from the Bible itself but are the theological beliefs that shape our approach as we pick up this text. They are like eyeglasses through which we see everything else but that we hardly notice wearing anymore because we have grown so used to them.

The sacred character of the Bible is summarized in our four Catholic beliefs about it, namely that

> God has had a special role in the production (inspiration) of these sacred books (canonical),
> which disclose God's own mysterious reality (revelation) without error (inerrancy).

When we identify the Bible as our sacred text, we are declaring our beliefs about the Bible. As Christians, we affirm that the Bible is not just another book. It is a collection of many texts of different literary forms, and it is not merely the product of human imagination and effort. While we recognize that the Bible was composed by human authors using their literary gifts to express their experience of God, we believe that God also cooperated in the production of the text so that these books contain a divine message.

This sacred character sets the Bible apart from all other books. Non-Christian believers have their own sacred books and their explanation of why their texts are sacred and how they ought to be interpreted. The sacred aspect of our Christian biblical text is summarized in four theological claims.

Claim 1: The Bible Is Inspired

Our first claim about the Bible as our sacred text is that its composition is inspired. *Inspiration* means "to breathe into." The image here is of God breathing into the author vital energy to write the ideas that express God's special meaning.

When we claim that the composition of the biblical books is inspired, we are saying that they are not merely human endeavors but that God somehow aided the human *authors to produce the text that God desired. We must always remember that believing the texts are inspired is a theological claim and not an explanation of the process.* We can make the assertion that something is true and yet not be able to explain exactly how it occurs.

A claim *that* something is true is not to be confused with an explanation of *how* it can be so. We know this from our own experience. For example, we know that our computer can handle thousands of tasks every second or that our car runs when we start it, without necessarily having a clue about how they work.

So in our theology we affirm that Jesus is truly human and truly divine, yet no theologian has provided a satisfactory explanation of how this mystery occurs. Through the claim

VATICAN II ON
THE TRAITS OF THE BIBLE AS A SACRED TEXT

The most authoritative Roman Catholic affirmations about the characteristics of the biblical text as revealed, inspired, inerrant in the truths of revelation, and canonical can be found in Vatican Council II's *Dogmatic Constitution on Divine Revelation (Dei Verbum).* The highlights of these Catholic affirmations are summarized here.

The Bible as our sacred text is:

1. *Revealed (DV #2): God's free self-communication for our salvation*

   "God chose to reveal Himself and to make known to us the hidden purpose of His will. . . . Through this revelation, therefore, the invisible God out of the abundance of His love speaks to humanity as friends and lives among them so that He might invite and take them into fellowship with Him. This plan of revelation is realized by deeds and words having an inner unity: the deeds wrought by God in the history of salvation manifest and confirm the teachings and realities signified by the words, while the words proclaim the deeds and clarify the mystery contained in them. By this revelation, then, the deepest truth about God and the salvation of humanity is made clear to us in Christ who is the mediator and at the same time the fullness of revelation."

Remember that God freely chose "to share those divine treasures which totally transcend the understanding of the human mind" (Vatican Council I, on Faith, ch. 2) (DV # 6). These truths alone can be identified as the truths of revelation.

of divine inspiration we affirm *that* God aided in the composition of the biblical text. But this is not a psychological description of *how* God influenced the writer. This will always remain shrouded in mystery.

2. *Inspired (DV #11): God's assistance to the human authors to write*

"Those divinely revealed realities which are contained and presented in sacred Scripture have been committed to writing under the inspiration of the Holy Spirit. Holy Mother Church, relying on the belief of the apostles, holds that the books of both the Old and New Testament in their entirety, with all their parts, are sacred and canonical because, having been written under the inspiration of the Holy Spirit they have God as their author and have been handed on as such to the Church herself. In composing the sacred books, God chose humans and while employed by God they made use of their powers and abilities, so that with God acting in them and through them, they, as true authors, consigned to writing everything and only those things which God wanted. Therefore, since everything asserted by the inspired authors or sacred writers must be held to be asserted by the Holy Spirit, it follows that the books of Scripture must be acknowledged as teaching firmly, faithfully, and without error that truth which God wanted put into the sacred writings for the sake of our salvation."

3. *Without error in the truths of our salvation (see quote under 2)*

4. *Canonical and normative for all members of the Church (see quote under 2)*

So sacred texts are designated by faith claims, supported by reason, and require a faith-oriented approach to guide the historical-critical and other methods used for interpreting their meaning (DV #12, and see especially the Pontifical Biblical Commission's 1993 document *The Interpretation of the Bible in the Church*) because encountering this text will transform our life (DV #21, 26).

We must also remember that when we are talking about biblical inspiration, we are talking about texts. Since all of the biblical books are inspired, we must understand that God has inspired many different types of literature — poetry,

WHY YOUR BIBLE IS DIFFERENT FROM OTHER BOOKS

narratives, proverbs, stories, letters, and historical documents. God communicates with us in a variety of inspired literary forms. As Vatican Council II reminds us, "truth is presented and expressed differently in historical, prophetic or poetic texts, or in other styles of speech" (*On Revelation,* no. 12). If we do not acknowledge this diversity of literary types, we run the risk of missing the message God desires to communicate to us. It is not enough to assume, as some people try to do, that everything in the Bible must be historical.

"All the senses of Holy Scripture are built on the literal sense, from which alone, and not from allegorical passages, can arguments be drawn. The spiritual sense brings nothing needful to faith which is not elsewhere clearly conveyed by the literal sense."

— *THOMAS AQUINAS*
Summa Theologiae, 1:1:10

Claim 2: The Bible Is Our Rule of Life

The Bible as a sacred text is the standard for our lives as Christian believers. The particular books collected as our Bible provide the fixed standard against which we measure the authenticity of our Christian faith. The Greek word for this standard or ruler is *canon.* So we describe these books as canonical. There are two characteristics of something that is canonical: First, it must be fixed as a standard; second, it can be used to measure other things.

For any standard to be effective, it has to be fixed and constant. Can you imagine trying to measure things with a ruler whose length is constantly changing? Thus the term canonical identifies only the books we include in the Bible. There are many other books that are as old as biblical books, but they are not included in the official list, the fixed standard, or canon, of Scripture.

Although we do not have the historical data to trace the process by which the early Christian community settled on just these particular books from among the many available, we do believe that the process was guided by God's Holy Spirit. We know that between the second and fourth centuries the Catholic canon, or official list of biblical books, was essentially decided.

This fixing of the canon allows all later Christians to measure their faith against the standard "rule" of the early communities. The designation of only these books as canonical does not deny that nonbiblical books can contain some truth about God or about the Christian life. Nor does it limit the developing theological reflection that over the centuries leads to more precise expressions of the biblical truths. The canon provides the basic standard against which the meaning and usefulness of these other books can be measured.

For us Christians, God is not only in the Bible but is also present and working in our lives. The biblical texts provide our most reliable clues as we discover and understand God's self-revelation in our world. The Bible is our most trustworthy guide to the knowledge of God's sacred reality and the most helpful source for the authentic responses we can make to God's transforming presence. With the help of these biblical clues, we can clarify our relationship with God and discover new ways to live it out.

"In discerning the canon of Scripture, the Church was also discerning and defining her own identity. Henceforth Scripture was to function as a mirror in which the Church could continually rediscover her identity and assess, century after century, the way in which she constantly responds to the gospel and equips herself to be an apt vehicle of its transmission. This confers on the canonical writings a salvific and theological value completely different from that attaching to other ancient texts. The latter may throw much light on the origins of the faith. But they can never substitute for the authority of the writings held to be canonical and thus fundamental for the understanding of the Christian faith."

— *THE PONTIFICAL BIBLICAL COMMISSION*
The Interpretation of the Bible in the Church (1993)

Claim 3: The Bible Is Revealed

Our third claim about the Bible as our sacred text is that its content or message is revealed. *Reveal* means "to take the veil off" or to uncover something that is hidden. We never know the thoughts or feelings of others unless they communicate to us in words or actions. Revelation unveils the hidden mystery of a person; we receive communication rather than a list of abstract truths. The Bible is described as God's self-revelation, or word, to us, which freely reveals the hidden mysteries of God's inner self.

When we claim that God uses these human texts to reveal, or uncover, for us the hidden mystery of God's self, we describe these texts as revealed. Texts are written communication. They are an extension of self-revelation because they disclose the mind of the author. Every text is a kind of revelation of the hidden depths of the author.

The Bible is our sacred text because it discloses, or reveals, God's personal mystery. We could never know this mystery without God's freely communicating it to us in ways we understand. Moreover, this self-disclosure never happens once and for all. It takes a lifetime of experience to get to know a human person well. We must expect that knowing well the mystery of God is a process that begins in our human lifetime but certainly does not end there.

Claim 4: The Bible Is Truthful

The final characteristic of the Bible as our sacred text is that it is without error in the divine truths that it reveals to us for our salvation. This claim of truth follows from the character of the text both as revealed and as inspired.

The truths of divine revelation are not something that we could learn about God by using our human intelligence. If we could discover these truths on our own, then God would not need to reveal them. Instead, these divinely revealed truths are something we would never have imagined, much less discovered by ourselves — the trinitarian reality of God and the incarnate, divine-human reality of Jesus of Nazareth. These core revelations are the foundation for all of our specifically Christian truths.

Theologians call these divinely revealed truths *mysteries.* A theological mystery describes something that our minds can never totally comprehend no matter how hard or how long we think about it. These mysteries are so profound that our human thinking will never explain them or exhaust their richness. Since they can come only from God as God's own self-revelation, we confidently affirm that they are without error.

"Being faithful to the Church, in fact, means resolutely finding one's place in the mainstream of the great Tradition that, under the guidance of the magisterium and assured of the Holy Spirit's special assistance, has recognized the canonical writings as the word addressed by God to his people and has never ceased meditating on them and discovering their inexhaustible riches."

— *POPE JOHN PAUL II*
Address to the Pontifical Biblical Commission (23 April 1993)

But since God chose to communicate these divine mysteries through the words of the biblical authors and inspire the process of composition so that the biblical books really do contain divine truths, we must carefully distinguish between the divine truth and the human truth found in them. We must accept the fact that even though their texts communicate divine revelation, the biblical authors were limited by their fallible and incomplete human knowledge concerning both historical events and God's own reality. So when we detect factual errors regarding human events or geography or anything the human authors did not accurately understand or express, these errors are the result of the limitations of the human authors rather than something God is responsible for. In the truth of God's divinely revealed mystery, there is no error.

As our sacred text, then, the Bible is our special source for discovering the God with whom we are intimately related. Through it, we are better able to encounter, recognize, understand, and respond to God. The Bible gives us a way to discern who God is, how God interacts with us, and what God expects from us as Christians in our relationship to God and to others.

Questions for Reflection and Group Discussion

1. *What is the difference between inspiration as a theological claim and as a psychological explanation?*
2. *For Christians, what is a revealed mystery? Why will we never fully comprehend it?*

3. *How would you explain to a friend that the inspired biblical authors could be wrong about historical or scientific information?*
4. *What is the canon of Scripture? How would you explain to a friend why it is limited to only certain books and not others?*

CHAPTER FOUR

Reading the Bible As a Catholic

The books of the Bible are a mysterious combination of divine and human composition. Their reality mirrors the divine-human composition of Jesus himself. As Vatican Council II expressed it in its *Dogmatic Constitution on Divine Revelation*, "Indeed, God's words, expressed through human language, have taken on the likeness of human speech, just as the Word of the eternal Father, when he assumed the flesh of human weakness, took on the likeness of human beings" (no. 13).

Just as we believe that Jesus was both fully divine and fully human, without mixture or confusion, we also believe that the Bible is both God's Word and human words. When we examine these writings, we will find that their fullest meaning can be comprehended only if we take seriously what both the human authors and God communicated. Errors occur when we put too much emphasis on either the divine or the human dimension — whether in regard to Jesus or the sacred Scriptures.

We can usually trace conflicts over Bible interpretation to an imbalance of emphasis. We can concentrate so emphatically on the divinity, or sacredness, of the Bible as "what God says" that we obscure its embodiment in our human language and situation. Or we can stress the human dimension of the Bible as "just another text" to the point of eliminating its divine character. In either case, the distinctive character of the Bible as a sacred text — God's Word in human language — is denied.

This need for a balanced approach stands behind the Church's diligent search not only for the literal meanings that the human authors intended but also for the spiritual meanings that God intended for our salvation. A Catholic interpretation of the Bible considers both of these dimensions in order to be faithful to the full reality of this sacred text.

In fact, we might best characterize this Catholic approach as a "faith-full" reading. Beginning from a standpoint of *faith,* the reader seeks to discover God by reading this sacred biblical text. But the reader also submits this text to the *full* spectrum of human techniques devised for reading and interpreting texts. Only this faith-full approach respects both the sacred and the textual dimensions of the Bible.

Recognizing the Bible as a Sacred Text

The sacred character of the Bible reminds us that the Bible is always about the mystery of God's own self. This sacred dimension reminds us of the discrepancy between our human condition and the divine reality to which the text refers. Since God is spiritual and invisible, descriptions of God in the Bible are not exact likenesses but human symbols.

"In the view of the Church, the Bible is not merely a literary work but also a religious work put together with a religious motive, chosen and constituted according to a religious criteria. . . . It differs from all human books for it is an inspired book containing and transmitting divine revelation."

— POPE PAUL VI
Address (19 April 1968)

The Bible expresses its sacred theological meaning in imaginative symbols that convey truths "beyond words" far better than reasoned arguments could. Since these divinely revealed mysteries are not objects, they cannot be spoken about directly or comprehended in ideas or concepts. What we learn about God in the Bible is never through direct description but rather through symbolic language. Thus, dealing with symbols becomes a necessary part of our reading task when we want to understand God's sacred reality.

Even though symbols of God always fall short of expressing fully the divine mystery, biblical authors depended on the evocative power of symbolic imagery to capture their experience of God's transcendent yet immanent presence. Learning to understand the sacred requires that we learn to interpret symbols. We trivialize the meaning of these symbols when we take them literalistically and treat them as if they were direct descriptions of God's divine reality.

The Bible's symbolic language wonderfully matches the elusive reality of God's mystery. Its vision and language reveal yet conceal, disclose yet obscure, and in the end leave incomprehensible the "depths of God" (1 Corinthians 2:10). Reaching up to this mystery from the depths of our humanity requires our best effort. Since there is always more than we can comprehend from our human perspective, we must return to the text over and over to be enriched by the treasures God has revealed to us. Because we are dealing with God's mystery, our Bible reading journey is never ending and full of surprises.

Recognizing the Bible as a Human Composition

Believers who accept the sacred character of the Bible text approach their reading and use of the text differently than do nonbelievers. But accepting the sacred character of the biblical text does not excuse us from following all the procedures demanded for skillful interpretation. The Bible may be a divinely inspired text, but our interpretations of it depend on our own reading skills and effort.

As a written text, the Bible works like any book. It is a human composition by an author for an audience in a particular place and time. It must be read by using various methods that careful and capable readers have devised. The biblical texts demand that we use all our skill to read and interpret properly the meanings inscribed within them. Reading and interpreting ancient texts also demand special attention to textual, historical, literary, and sociopolitical issues. To read texts adequately, we must consider all of these historical and critical factors.

Perhaps the most important factor we must deal with is the gap between the past and the present. When the text was first written, the author and readers shared the same situation. Interpreting what the author meant was not as difficult in this shared world. When an author and audience share the same world of experience, fewer presuppositions are needed to discover the meaning that the author is trying to communicate. This is why reading our daily newspaper or a contemporary novel seems so effortless.

But as the ancient world of the author (then) and that of later readers (now) become distanced either by history or by culture (or, in the case of the Bible, both), difficulties in reading emerge.

In the nineteenth century, a major shift in our thinking began when Napoleon's conquest of Egypt brought European scholars to a brand-new awareness. They were overwhelmed by the realization that the past was not just an earlier version of today but that the peoples and cultures of the past were *essentially different* from those of the present. To deal with this new awareness of history, scholars devised, and have continued to refine, methods of exploring history by using ancient texts in order to bridge the historical gap between the present and the past.

In the twentieth century, another important shift occurred in our understanding of culture. As anthropologists traveled the globe observing all the various peoples and their ways of life, they concluded that culture is not something some people have and others do not. They recognized that every group, no matter how "primitive," has a culture or system around which it organizes its life as a society. Since culture is essential for human existence, it appears in various forms in every human community.

These two pivotal changes have had tremendous effects on our approach to reading and interpreting the Bible. We now know that for an adequate reading or interpretation of a text, we must understand the historical and cultural situation of the original author and audience. This method, which searches for what the text meant in its original situation, is

DECIDING TO MAKE YOUR JOURNEY

called the historical-critical method. Only through the use of this method can we hope to bridge the chasm that separates the ancient historical and cultural world of the author and the modern technological and cultural world of today's readers.

The Catholic Approach:
Seeking Both the Divine and Human Meanings

Our Catholic beliefs, which affirm what we consider to be true about the Bible, distinguish our approach from that of non-believers. The category of "nonbelievers" includes not only those from non-Christian religious traditions but also literary critics who appreciate the Bible only as influential literature and scientific historians who share no conviction about the Bible's religious truths. Our approach also differs from naively literalistic readers who do not acknowledge any historical or cultural distance between the ancient situation and our own. Finally, our Catholic approach differs from the approach of readers who deny or downplay the role of community tradition in the transmission and interpretation of divine revelation.

Our Catholic approach deliberately reads the Bible in relation to our Church's tradition. We do not believe that all truth is found in the Bible. But we do believe that the truth that is found there is especially significant because it reveals God's hidden mystery and what God wants for us and our world.

Within the Catholic tradition, the Bible has never been considered a document meant only for scholarly examination. From the beginning, Scripture was used to clarify and deepen our relationship with God and with one another. Whatever the fruits of scholarship might be, they become useful when they serve to help our relationship with God.

When we read "within the tradition," we accept the guidance of the community and not just our individual, private reading. The Bible was the Church's book long before it became ours! So to read the Bible as a Catholic means to be aware, at least in general, of the guidelines that the Church has provided. These guidelines come to us through the Church's formal teachings or statements about Scripture and by the use of Scripture in other documents and in the Church's worship. These Church guidelines have always stressed the need for balance in attending to both the sacred and the human dimensions of the biblical text.

Early Guidelines from Church Practice

Because the Church has always considered the Bible to be more than merely a history book or a literary text, it has always demanded that we use more than historical and literary techniques for reading and interpretation. That is, if we are to discover the sacred or fuller meaning of Scripture, we must go beyond mere historical and literary study.

The Church has always read the Bible as a book whose meaning cannot be exhausted by scholarly investigation. Because of this, the Church has never considered that the literal sense—the human author's intended meaning—encompasses all that the Bible means. As God's revealed Word, the Bible refers to a more-than-human reality. Thus it can legitimately be interpreted in ways that are grounded in the literal sense but go beyond it.

In order to get beyond the literal or historical level of meaning, early Church interpreters from Paul onward resorted to interpreting the Bible in a symbolic way. The basic assumption was that the biblical words referred not merely to the human realities that they described but to invisible divine realities as well. The Bible was understood as an extended symbol, or allegory, that connected the biblical text and the divine reality of God. Allegorical methods were devised to discover these fuller spiritual meanings.

"God can be known to us in the same way as persons can see an endless ocean by standing at the shore at night with a dimly lit candle. Do you think they can see much? Not much, almost nothing. And, nevertheless, they see the water well. They know that there is an ocean in front of them, that this ocean is huge and that they cannot see it all at once. The same is true of our knowledge of God."

—*ST. SIMEON THE NEW THEOLOGIAN*
Oration 61 (ca. A.D. 1000)

These allegorical methods worked by connecting details from biblical persons, events, and themes with later persons and events. As connections were made, new and surprising meanings emerged. For example, for the early Christians, events from the Old Testament story of God's relationship with the Jews became types, or models, that foreshadowed later events in the New Testament story of God's relationship with the Christians. So Jesus could be understood by seeing him as the fulfillment of the Old Testament persons. He was a new Moses, a new David, a new Solomon, a prophet like Elijah.

As more complicated problems arose and simple allegory was no longer adequate, more sophisticated ways of seeking the spiritual meanings were developed. Throughout the Middle Ages, the desire to go beyond the literal sense that the human author intended took the form of more precise and elaborate methods. Students learned these methods and remembered them through the use of a famous Latin couplet:

> *Littera gesta docet, quid credas allegoria*
> *Moralis quid agas, quo tendas anagogia.*
> ("The literal sense shows what happened, the allegorical what you are to believe, the moral what you are to do, the anagogical where you are headed.")

The literal sense concerns the events described in the text. In their prescientific understanding of history, medieval scholars assumed these events to be directly factual and thus the foundation for all the other meanings. Once literal meanings were understood, further spiritual meanings could be derived because the literal sense pointed to divine events outside the text.

This connection of text and divine events is the foundation of the allegorical sense, which somehow relates everything in the text to the reality of Christ. Allegory shows us what we are to believe in that everything points to Christ and his redemptive mission. This allegorical sense unfolds the spiritual meaning of Scripture by showing us the connection between the biblical text and Christ.

Another spiritual sense is the moral sense, which shows us what we are to do. Since God constantly calls us to conversion, this moral meaning points us toward our own response to God's mystery in our lives. The events of Jesus' life become the pattern for our life. By applying the moral sense of a text, we become aware of how God is saving us through Christ and what we ought to do in response.

The final aspect of the spiritual sense is the anagogical sense, which shows us where we are going. The word *anagogical* means "leading upward" and indicates the final heavenly goal toward which we strive. This meaning serves to build up our hope.

There are many examples of these four senses, or meanings, of Scripture, but a simple one is the four ways of looking at the city of Jerusalem. The literal sense understands Jerusalem

READING THE BIBLE AS A CATHOLIC

as a historical city; the allegorical sense understands Jerusalem as the Church; the moral sense understands Jerusalem as the Christian soul; and the anagogical sense understands Jerusalem as the heavenly city.

This fourfold method dominated the interpretation of texts until the rise of the more scientific and historical techniques devised in the nineteenth century for the under-standing of ancient texts. These newer methods caused much controversy and were only slowly approved and encouraged by the Church. This confrontation between the Church and the scientifically based, historical-critical scholars about how to interpret the Bible has been a dominant issue for the last two centuries.

Modern Catholic Guidelines for Scripture Interpretation

As mentioned earlier, a major controversy over the use of modern scientific and historical methods for examining the biblical texts rocked the Church in the nineteenth century. The nineteenth century was a difficult time both politically and intellectually for the Catholic Church. Beginning with the French Revolution (1789), bitter disagreements had sev-ered the relationship between church and state, which had endured in Europe for roughly fifteen hundred years (since the Roman emperor Constantine recognized Christianity as a religion in A.D. 313). Responding to the hostility directed toward it, the Church assumed an equally hostile attitude toward the modern world and the changes it was bringing.

By the 1890s, Italian nationalism had so drastically restricted the Church's political power that the Church's voice was limited to issues of private morality, not public politics. In the intellectual field, the experimental method of science had become the model of all human knowing. Since scientific thinking was equated with reason, faith was discounted as irrational and considered merely a matter of personal feeling. Scientific methods of biblical scholarship, not faith, were considered the best way of determining the Bible's meaning.

In 1893, Pope Leo XIII wrote the first modern papal letter, or encyclical, offering specific directives about the Catholic approach to Scripture. His letter, called *Providentissimus Deus* (A Most Provident God), attempted to initiate a cautious reconciliation between the tradition of Catholic biblical scholarship and the developing scientific approach to biblical criticism.

Leo respected learning and wanted Bible scholars to use what was best in the new scientific approaches but also to be aware of the dangers that led scholars to positions contrary to the Church's doctrine. His proposals guided Catholic scholars through the difficult years of the first half of the twentieth century.

Leo desired to encourage biblical scholars, and his letter inaugurated a modern dialogue between Catholic biblical scholarship and the scientific methods of reading texts. Although his primary emphasis was on using scholarship to defend against attacks on the faith, Leo also stressed the need to search for the meaning of the biblical texts. He encouraged careful historical investigation of the origin and transmission of biblical writings. He also recognized that there are depths of meaning that even the original authors might not have perceived. He encouraged Catholic scholars to rely on not merely the Latin translation of the Bible that had been used for almost fifteen centuries but also to investigate the Hebrew and Greek versions.

"The language of the Bible is employed to express, under the inspiration of the Holy Ghost, many things which are beyond the power and scope of human reason — that is to say, divine mysteries and all that is related to them. There is sometimes in such passages a fullness and a hidden depth of meaning which the letter hardly expresses and which the laws of interpretation hardly warrant. Moreover, the literal sense itself frequently admits other senses, adapted to illustrate dogma or to confirm morality."

— *POPE LEO XIII*
Encyclical "Providentissimus Deus" (1893)

In 1943, to celebrate the fiftieth anniversary of Leo's letter, Pope Pius XII wrote a commemorative encyclical letter called *Divino Afflante Spiritu* (Inspired by the Divine Spirit). This letter carries Leo's cautious beginnings to a full-fledged endorsement of the use of modern scholarly methods for interpreting Scripture. In particular, Pius not only encouraged but also required scholars to use the biblical texts in their original Hebrew, Aramaic, and Greek languages, together with a careful historical and literary study to determine their genuine meaning. This approach demanded both an understanding of the author's intended meaning (the literal sense — but notice that this is rather different from the medieval literal sense, which referred to the text's description of events) and an awareness of the deeper theological meanings (the spiritual sense) relevant to the Church's traditional doctrines and moral teaching.

This letter fostered an enormous revival of Catholic interest in Scripture. Using the modern methods endorsed by the pope, Catholic biblical scholars finally began to take their place among the foremost Scripture scholars in the world. Their books and articles, together with new and more accurate Catholic translations of the Bible, opened up to the laity the long-neglected riches of Scripture.

The Church's cautious approval of historical scholarship as the necessary tool for unlocking the meaning of Scripture culminated in the *Dogmatic Constitution on Divine Revelation (Dei Verbum)* of Vatican Council II (1962 – 65). With the highest degree of teaching authority, this Council solemnly defined the basic teaching of the Church on the Bible and how it must be interpreted. This document, more than any other, invites us to step confidently into the future from the firm foundation of the trustworthy guidelines accumulated from our whole past tradition. Reading this document is the best way to learn what the Church teaches about Scripture and how to interpret it.

This conciliar teaching of Vatican II was elaborated on by the Pontifical Biblical Commission (the official group of Scripture scholars chosen by the Pope to help the teaching office in biblical matters) in their *Interpretation of the Bible in the Church* (1993). This publication commemorated the hundredth anniversary of Pope Leo's letter promoting modern biblical studies. In this important document, the commission describes in detail the various modern scholarly methods and approaches for interpreting Scripture and evaluates their specific contributions and dangers.

The methods and approaches of biblical scholarship grow out of the diverse questions that curious and competent readers ask of the texts. Each *method,* or approach, arises to solve specific questions and concerns. The word *method* means a way of getting from "here" to "there." Methods of Bible interpretation help us get from the strange, ancient world with its unfamiliar language, customs, and ideas, to our present world.

The Pontifical Biblical Commission reminds us that there is, strictly speaking, no Catholic method of scriptural inter-pretation. There is a Catholic approach, however, which links the biblical text to the tradition of the Church and holds together our modern scientific culture and the Judeo-Christian religious tradition. The Catholic approach also demands, as the context for all understanding, a faith perspective that is rooted in a relationship with God.

During the last half-century God's Word has been opened to all the faithful in an unprecedented way. Thanks to the promotion of biblical studies by Popes Leo and Pius and the bishops of Vatican Council II, we have the chance to hear God's Word with reverence and proclaim it with faith in ways that were practically impossible just a century ago.

Throughout the centuries the Church's guidelines have followed the broad middle path of tried-and-true methods of interpretation. As in so many other areas, the Church was seldom first to devise new interpretive methods or to approve them. The Church's teaching office was content to "make haste slowly" and test things before approving them. Like a skilled river pilot on the Mississippi, the Church's guidelines recognize that dangers lurk most often when one slips out of the main channel and glides into the shallows near the shore. Whether one moves too far to the right toward naively spiritual readings or to the left toward simply historical readings, the religious results can be disastrous. The safe passage is always in the deep and smooth-running channel where both dimensions are affirmed.

READING THE BIBLE AS A CATHOLIC

> "[In Scripture], truth is just as much opposed by an adulteration of its meaning as by a corruption of its text. . . . One person perverts the Scriptures with his hand, another their meaning by his interpretation."
>
> — *TERTULLIAN*
> *On Prescription of Heretics,* chapters 17, 39 (ca. A.D. 207)

Moreover, since the Church was always primarily concerned with the demands of practical life and worship rather than with mere scholarship, no matter how theoretically brilliant the methods and conclusions of secular scholarship might have been, the Church carefully evaluated them in the light of its mission to guard and proclaim the gospel truth.

Questions for Reflection and Group Discussion

1. *Explain to a friend why our Catholic beliefs about Scripture guide our Catholic approach to reading it.*
2. *Why does our modern sense of history demand more specialized methods for understanding ancient texts?*
3. *Explain the difference between what we usually mean when we say, "take something literally" and what biblical scholars mean when they seek the Bible's "literal sense."*
4. *Using the fourfold senses of Scripture, how might you interpret the meaning of Mary, the mother of God? Or the cross of Jesus?*

PART TWO

Preparing for Your Journey

In Paul we read about Christ: "In whom are hidden all the treasures of wisdom and knowledge." See what he says; all the treasures of wisdom and knowledge. Not that some are and some are not; but all the treasures of wisdom and knowledge, but they are hidden. So what is in Him is not lacking to Him, even though it be hidden from us.

But if all the treasures of wisdom and knowledge are hidden in Christ, we must ask why they are hidden. It is our part to seek, His to grant what we ask, ours to make a beginning, His to bring it to completion, ours to offer what we can, His to finish what we cannot.

— *ST. JEROME,*
Dialogue against Pelagius (A.D. 415)

CHAPTER FIVE

Getting the Lay of the Land: A Map and Compass for Your Journey

We would never travel to a new country without first having some idea of its terrain. To do this, we rely first on general topographical maps that show the geographical configurations of mountains, plains, coastlines, and major rivers. Then we find our way using more detailed maps that show cities, towns, and their connecting roads. Our reading journey also requires some awareness of the Bible's topography — how it all fits together structurally — and then more detailed directives for helping us along specific paths.

In unfamiliar countryside, we might also need a compass to fix our location and keep our orientation constantly on target. Just as a compass works on coordinates to determine our location by triangulation, so we can fix our attention on the three essentials of the communication situation — the author, the audience, and the text that mediates between them. We will always have some basic questions in these areas to keep ourselves properly directed for our journey.

A Map of Our Bible's Overall Structure

The two great divisions in our Christian Bible are the Old Testament and the New Testament. The Old Testament is the collection of sacred books that the early Christians adopted from Judaism. The New Testament is the collection of our specifically Christian writings. The word *testament* here is the older English word for a covenant relationship.

Since many scholars today think that the old / new designation has negative connotations, they are experimenting with other "value-free" terminology. So in some books you might find the Old Testament called the First or Prior Testament and the New Testament called the Second or Later Testament. Others draw the distinction between the Hebrew, or Jewish, Scriptures and the Christian Scriptures. Nevertheless, the more familiar terms *old* and *new* still remain the most conventional way of designating the Bible's major parts.

The Christian Old Testament

The Christian Old Testament is adapted from the Jewish sacred Scriptures. The Jews divided their sacred texts into three general categories: The Law (Torah), the Prophets (Nevi'im), and the Writings (Ketuvim). In Hebrew, the first letters of these terms form the acronym Tanakh, which is what Jewish scholars prefer to call the Old Testament.

So in the time of Jesus, one could refer to the Bible as the law, the prophets, and the psalms (Luke 24:44) or as the law and the prophets (see, for example, Matthew 5:17; 7:12;

A MAP OF THE JEWISH BIBLE

The Law (Torah)	The Prophets (Nevi'im)		The Writings (Ketuvim)
5 BOOKS	**8 BOOKS**		**11 BOOKS**
Genesis	Former	Latter	BOOKS OF TRUTH ('EMETH)
Exodus	Joshua	Isaiah	Psalms
Leviticus	Judges	Jeremiah	Proverbs
Numbers	1 and 2 Samuel	Ezekiel	Job
Deuteronomy	1 and 2 Kings	THE TWELVE	THE FIVE SCROLLS (MEGILLOTH)
		Hosea	Solomon's Song
		Joel	Ruth
		Amos	Lamentations
		Obadiah	Ecclesiastes
		Jonah	Esther
		Micah	
		Nahum	Daniel
		Habakkuk	Ezra-Nehemiah
		Zephaniah	1 and 2 Chronicles
		Haggai	
		Zechariah	
		Malachi	

GETTING THE LAY OF THE LAND

22:40; John 1:45; Acts 13:15; 24:14; 28:23; Romans 3:21), or, more simply, as just the law (Luke 10:26; John 10:34).

Early Christians used these three general groupings but rearranged their order so that the Prophets would come last. In this way the Old Testament seemed to point directly to the coming of Christ that was recorded in the New Testament. When the Bible was translated into Latin, the order of books was further modified into the arrangement found in our modern Bible. The three Jewish groups of books are now redistributed into four sections — the Pentateuch, the historical books, the wisdom books, and the prophetic books.

The Pentateuch (from the Greek word for "five scrolls or books") contains the first five books of the Bible. These are the same books that the Jews call the Law or Torah (Hebrew for "instruction"). They narrate the basic story of God's search for an appropriate covenant partner, from the creation of Adam to Abraham to Abraham's descendants in Egypt under Moses. About 1250 B.C., God liberated these people from their oppression in Egypt and led them for forty years through the wilderness until they reached the Promised Land.

Woven into these narratives are descriptions of the covenant ceremonies and the detailed law codes that instructed the people about their behavior in relation to God and to one another. The Pentateuch as we have it in our Bibles, which assumed its final form about four hundred years before Christ, reflects the results of several centuries of Jewish editing.

A MAP OF THE CATHOLIC BIBLE

The Old Testament (46 Books)

Pentateuch
Genesis
Exodus
Leviticus
Numbers
Deuteronomy

Historical Books
Joshua
Judges
Ruth
1 and 2 Samuel
1 and 2 Kings
1 and 2 Chronicles
Ezra
Nehemiah
Tobit*
Judith*
Esther
1 and 2 Maccabees*

Wisdom Books
Job
Psalms
Proverbs

Ecclesiastes
Song of Songs
Wisdom*
Sirach
  (Ecclesiasticus)*

Prophetic Books
Isaiah
Jeremiah
Lamentations
Baruch*
Ezekiel
Daniel
Hosea
Joel
Amos
Obadiah
Jonah
Micah
Nahum
Habakkuk
Zephaniah
Haggai
Zechariah
Malachi

The New Testament (27 books)

Gospels
Matthew
Mark
Luke
John
Acts of the Apostles

Pauline Letters
Romans
1 and 2 Corinthians
Galatians
Ephesians
Philippians
Colossians
1 and 2 Thessalonians
1 and 2 Timothy
Titus
Philemon
Hebrews

Catholic Letters
James
1 and 2 Peter
1, 2, and 3 John
Jude
Revelation

* indicates a Catholic deuterocanonical book, which Protestants consider noncanonical and do not include in their Bibles, except sometimes in a special section called the Apocrypha.

GETTING THE LAY OF THE LAND

Then come the sixteen historical books that tell the story of Israel during the millennium before Christ. "Historical" is a traditional label rather than a scholarly conclusion. The books of Tobit, Esther, and Judith, for example, are fictionalized narratives that demonstrate how ancient historians taught their audiences by providing examples rather than establishing "facts" the way historians do today.

In this historical section, the books of Joshua and Judges recount the experiences of the Jewish people in the two centuries beginning with their entry into the Promised Land and ending with the founding of the kingdom under Saul. The books of Samuel and Kings continue the story by focusing on the kings who ruled between approximately 1000 B.C. and 587 B.C., when the Jewish kingdom was destroyed by the Babylonian Empire and the leaders were sent into exile for fifty years.

The books of Chronicles retell the history given in Samuel and Kings to explain how God allowed the exile. Ezra and Nehemiah recount the people's heroic efforts of restoration after the exile. Finally, the books of Maccabees tell of the people's resistance and revolt against their Greek overlords during the second century before Christ.

The historical books are followed by the seven wisdom books. Job, Proverbs, Ecclesiastes, Wisdom, and Sirach contain the truths and truisms that constituted the foundation for a worldly education among the elite. Parts of these books have parallels in Egyptian and other ancient Near Eastern literature. The poetic Song of Songs is a love song attributed to King Solomon. The book of Psalms is a collection of 150 songs that were used for Jewish worship. They express the spectrum of emotions of the people in relationship with God.

The final section of our Old Testament has eighteen books of prophets. Although the books are not grouped chronologically, their work spans the period from about 750 B.C. to 350 B.C. The longest books are those of the four major prophets — Isaiah, Jeremiah, Ezekiel, and Daniel along with Lamentations, considered to be written by Jeremiah, and Baruch, written by Jeremiah's secretary. Then the twelve books of the minor prophets gather together the wide variety and styles of prophetic messages from God to the Jewish people. These are "minor" not in importance but only because they are shorter in length than the books of the major prophets.

The New Testament

All Christian Bibles have the same number (twenty-seven) and arrangement of the New Testament books. They include the four Gospels, in the traditional order of Matthew, Mark, Luke, and John. Matthew is first because it was supposed that this Gospel was originally composed in Aramaic before it was translated into the Greek version we have today. Most scholars now think that Mark was the first Gospel written.

> "It is important for every Catholic to realize that the Church produced the New Testament, not vice versa. The Bible did not come down from heaven, whole and intact, given by the Holy Spirit. Just as the experience and faith of Israel developed its sacred books, so was the early Christian Church the matrix of the New Testament. . . . The Bible, then, is the Church's book. The New Testament did not come before the Church, but from the Church."
>
> — *U.S. BISHOPS*
> "A Pastoral Statement for Catholics on Biblical Fundamentalism" (1987)

Then comes the Acts of the Apostles, which is actually the companion volume to Luke's Gospel (a connection that is usually missed because our organization separates them). After the Gospels come the letters, beginning with those of Paul (arranged in the order of length), then the other pastoral and catholic letters. The final book is that of Revelation, or Apocalypse (the Greek word for "revelation").

Why Catholic and Protestant Old Testaments Differ

Although Catholic and Protestant Old Testaments are arranged in the same four groups (law, prophets, wisdom, history), the number of books in each group differs. Catholic Bibles have forty-six Old Testament books, and Protestant Bibles have thirty-nine. Catholics and Protestants do not agree on the same canon, and each denomination labels books from the viewpoint of its own canon. Books that belong inside the canon are called canonical. Those that are outside the canon are called apocryphal (from the Greek word meaning "hidden"). There are thirty-nine books that Catholics and Protestants agree are canonical. There are many other books that both groups reject from their canons and label as apocryphal.

But there are seven books and parts of two others that are disputed. Catholics include them as canonical; Protestants reject them as apocryphal. These seven books — Wisdom, Sirach, Baruch, 1 and 2 Maccabees, Tobit, Judith, and parts of Daniel — are called deuterocanonical (Greek for "second canon"), meaning that they are canonical but that their right to be in the canon has often been disputed.

The dispute rests on several factors. Until the second and third centuries after Christ, there was no firmly established and universally agreed-upon list of sacred books that formed the Jewish canon. So in the first century there existed among Jews — and consequently among Christians — discrepancies about what belonged in the canon and what did not.

Jews in the Palestinian homeland accepted as sacred only books in the Hebrew language. But Jews outside of the homeland, who relied on the Greek translation of the Jewish Scriptures called the Septuagint, included some books in Greek or Aramaic that the Hebrew purists would not recognize as sacred Scripture. Thus when Greek-speaking Christians (who by the end of the first century constituted the majority of Christians) adopted the Septuagint translation of the Old Testament, they also accepted its extra books.

In the fourth century, when St. Jerome translated the Bible into Latin, he too included the Greek Septuagint number of books. So for the next thousand years — until the Protestant Reformation in the sixteenth century — the number and arrangement of books in the Old Testament, as accepted in Roman Catholic Christianity, remained constant.

When the discrepancy between the Hebrew canon and the Greek canon was rediscovered in the sixteenth century, many Protestant churches opted to follow the Hebrew canon rather than the Greek. So they removed these seven deutero-canonical books from their Bibles. However, they often included them in an appendix, which Protestants still do today.

Signposts along the Way: Chapter and Verse

The Bible text we have now is carefully marked with helpful trail markers. But before the Bible began to be printed in standardized form, finding your place in a handwritten manuscript was very difficult. Since every handwritten text was different, a reader would have to know the particular manuscript to find where the text for the day began. Before reading, especially for the liturgy, the reader would have to prepare the reading to determine exactly what the text said. Although this seems strange to us, it was absolutely necessary because ancient scrolls contained few aids for reading, such as punctuation, word divisions, or paragraphs.

In Hebrew texts, words were separated, but the vowels were not written. Thus reading the text out loud was the first and most basic form of interpretation. Until the words were vocalized, the vowels were indefinite, and the meaning remained ambiguous. For example, if we did the same thing in English, we might come across the sentence: LRD S GD FR JWS. By supplying the vowels for these consonants, we could come up with "The Lord is God for Jews" or "Lard is good for jaws." Only the context of the words would allow us to decide which meaning was most accurate.

Unlike Hebrew texts, Greek texts included vowels but were written in capital letters without any breaks between words. Imagine how hard it would be to read a text like this: GODWASRECONCILINGTHEWORLDTOHIMSELFIN-CHRISTNOTCOUNTINGTHEIRTRESPASSESAGAINST-THEMANDENTRUSTINGTOUSTHEMESSAGEOFRECON-CILIATION (2 Corinthians 5:19, NAB). To help their oral performance, ancient readers marked off the breaks between words with tiny dots, or "points." These "pointed texts" now provide clues for scholars about the most intelligible division of texts into words.

Once books were printed, rather than hand copied, the format of the text was greatly standardized. Longer texts could be broken down into sections, chapters, and then into smaller units called verses. Thus the whole Bible could be easily navigated by knowing which book, chapter, and verse you were reading. Cross-referencing became easier because one could simply identify any quotation by its chapter and verse.

DECIPHERING A BIBLICAL CITATION

Gen 4	Genesis, chapter 4
Gen 4:3	Genesis, chapter 4, verse 3
Gen 4:3 – 11	Genesis, chapter 4, verses 3 through 11
Gen 4:3, 11	Genesis chapter 4, verses 3 and 11
Gen 4:3 – 11:1	Genesis, chapter 4, verse 3 through chapter 11, verse 1

Today the books of the Bible are usually abbreviated. Look at the introductory material in your Bible to find the specific abbreviations it uses. Annotated Bibles contain many other supplementary helps for readers. These often include introductions to the books, chapter or paragraph headings that help us find our way, cross-references to similar passages of Scripture, and scholarly footnotes to help with the difficult passages.

Remember that these extra helps are not part of the sacred text and cannot be treated as revealed, inspired, or inerrant. They are only as reliable and trustworthy as the scholars who provide them. The most important advantage of using an annotated Bible is that if the notes are done well, we have immediate help with problematic passages and do not have to stop our reading to go search for information. You will be surprised how often your questions will be answered because the scholars have already tackled them.

Our Compass for Orientation: Essential Questions

In unfamiliar territory, a compass helps us locate where we are and find our way. The compass works because it is constantly oriented to the North Pole. For our Bible journey, our coordinates are the six essential questions that must be answered about any text. They can be summarized like this:

Who (the author)
addresses whom (the audience)
in what circumstances (the situation)
in what way (form)
with what message (content)
for what reason (function)?

Ordinarily, the introduction to each biblical book gives enough background that you can to read it with an awareness of what the biblical author intended to communicate to the original audience. These introductions usually provide a brief summary of the scholarly conclusions about the identity of the author and the original audience, their historical situation, why the book was written, what literary form was used, and a summary of the book's content and message.

Historical Issues	Critical Issues
Who (the author)	With what message (content)
addresses whom (the audience)	in what way (form)
in what circumstances (the situation)	for what reason (function)

Every reader must be aware of these questions as he or she seeks to understand the meaning of the text. If these questions are neglected or inadequately answered, readers can easily lose their way or come up with meanings that the author never intended to communicate. Even small errors can affect how we interpret what we read, much like being a few compass degrees off may seem insignificant at first but can drastically change where we end up after miles of traveling.

Questions for Reflection and Group Discussion

1. *Why would Christians call the Jewish Scriptures the Old Testament and the Christian Scriptures the New Testament? What does this terminology reveal about the Jews' and Christians' differing viewpoints on their relationship with God?*

2. *Explain to a Protestant friend why his or her Bible does not have the same books as your Catholic Bible.*

3. *What do Catholics mean when they use the terms* apocryphal *and* deuterocanonical?

4. *Find the following references in your Bible: Ps 85:9; Lk 8:21; Ex 24:1 – 11; Dt 17:14 – 20; Neh 8; Is 52:13 – 53:12; Mt 5 – 7; 2 Pt 3:8; Est A12 (NAB); Jer 12:7 – 13; Eccl 12:11 – 13.*

CHAPTER SIX

How the Bible Came to Be: From Scrolls to Book

Our conveniently bound Bible is really a collection of books that comes to us translated from its various original languages. This would have been immediately obvious to the Jews and earliest Christians, whose Scriptures would have consisted of a closet full of papyrus rolls. Each one would have been wrapped up and tied with a separate piece of papyrus to identify the scroll, just as a dust jacket does today. This would help readers find the scroll they wanted to read in their community gathering.

Books in the ancient world were published by copying them individually by hand (hence, the word *manuscript*). Because there was no such thing as copyright, authors usually expected and even encouraged the reproduction of their writings. Authors wrote primarily for honor and fame rather than for money, and reproductions of their manuscripts enhanced their reputations.

"I make no attempt to conceal it. Except for the Scriptures, the order of whose words is a mystery, I never translate the Greek word for word. I express the meaning. On that I can cite the example of Cicero when he translated. . . . Horace, too, that shrewd and scholarly figure, gives the same advice to a translator in his *Ars Poetica,* 'It is not word for word that a translator interprets.'"

— *ST. JEROME*
Letter 57

A manuscript was usually available to almost anyone who wished to make a copy. Of course, the quality of the copies often varied, depending on the skill of the copyist. Consequently, no two manuscripts were alike. The size of the handwriting and the arrangement of material on the page often differed, and there were mistakes in copying as well as deliberate changes to the text. For purposes of reference or copying, authors often kept an authentic version of their work in the private library of their patron or in a more public city library or church archive.

What Manuscripts Do We Have?

We do not have the original manuscript (called an autograph) of any biblical book, only copies of copies of copies. But Bible scholars have at their disposal more manuscripts of the Bible than of any other ancient document. For the New Testament, there are more than five thousand manuscripts in Greek, eight thousand in Latin, and one thousand in other languages. These sources vary; some are but tiny fragments of a few words, and others contain the whole New Testament. Until fifty years ago, our oldest manuscripts of the Old Testament dated back only about a thousand years. But thanks to recent discoveries, our oldest manuscripts now include more than two hundred from the period of about 250 B.C. to A.D. 135.

The most famous of these are the Dead Sea Scrolls, which were found in Palestine in 1947 at Qumran near the Dead Sea. These manuscripts had been hidden in caves cut into the cliffs. They are almost a thousand years older than any Old Testament manuscripts scholars had ever been able to use in the translation of the text. They include either the whole or part of almost every Old Testament book, commentaries on biblical books, and other writings that scholars think were probably part of the library of the Essene community. These Jewish sectarians lived in a kind of monastery at Qumran, which was destroyed in A.D. 68 by the Romans.

By leaping back almost a thousand years in manuscript evidence to the first century, scholars have reinforced their confidence in the Hebrew text they have relied on for modern translations. The close similarity of these newly discovered texts to later copies demonstrates how carefully and accurately the Hebrew text was preserved through twenty-plus centuries of copying. When scholars compared the modern Hebrew text with these ancient ones, they confirmed how close the modern Old Testament is to the text discovered in the Dead Sea Scrolls.

The task of textual scholars is to comb through these thousands of surviving manuscripts to determine their types, their dates of composition, the extent of their geographical distribution, and the relationships that exist among similar manuscripts. In particular, scholars are interested in which manuscript was copied from which and how variations introduced by one manuscript got transmitted to later copies. Scholars compare the numerous textual variations to identify which ones were unintentional and which ones were intentionally introduced by the copyists. The goal of all this textual study is to approximate as closely as possible what they think was the original version of the text.

The text of the Bible that we rely on today for our translations does not directly correspond to any single ancient manuscript. It has been pieced together using thousands of scholarly judgments about what the original text must have been. Despite all these textual variations, the amazing thing is that no essential Christian truth or doctrine has been put in doubt by any of these manuscript differences.

What Do Manuscripts Look Like?

The original manuscripts of the Bible were probably written on papyrus. Papyrus looks much like a slightly stiffer version of our modern paper. Papyrus plants grow plentifully in the marshy areas of the Nile River in Egypt. The stalk, triangular in shape and ten to twelve feet long, can easily be stripped and its pithy center (called *biblos* in Greek) cut into small strips. These strips are then laid on a flat surface, first vertically and then horizontally. The two layers are then pressed, dried, and smoothed with a shell to create a single sheet usually six to nine inches high and twelve to eighteen inches wide.

Several sheets (typically about twenty) would then be slightly overlapped and pressed together to form a roll. For a longer text, several rolls could be strung together to make a scroll (*biblion* in Greek). The maximum length for a scroll before it became completely unwieldy for the reader to roll and unroll was about thirty feet. Matthew's Gospel, for example, would fill a scroll of about this length.

Writing was usually done only on the horizontally laid side, and the scroll was rolled so that the writing was inside. Occasionally, either because papyrus was lacking or because the author had so much to say, scrolls were written on both sides. (See the book of Revelation 5:1. God's scroll was double-sided and fastened with seven wax seals.)

The unwieldy character of larger scrolls probably led the early Christians to adopt the codex, or leaf, form of books instead of the more common scrolls. Originally, the codex was made by hinging together blocks of wood. The blocks were hollowed out in the center, and wax was put into the hollow part. The wax was written on, then smoothed out so that it could be used over and over. Two blocks hinged together made a codex. The wax erased easily and so made a good learning tool for students practicing their writing. A codex of papyrus was made by folding the sheets down the middle and sewing them together at the fold, much like our modern books are made.

Several advantages of the codex might have made it preferable to the scroll. First, the length of the book was no longer restricted to a set length, as it was in the scroll form. A codex could encompass more material simply by adding more and more pages. What was impossible for the scroll was now possible in this new format. The entire Bible, for example, could be put together into a single large codex.

Second, since both sides of the pages were used, the codex was more economical. Since both sides of the sheet could be written on, fewer sheets needed to be purchased. More text could be fitted onto fewer pages, and thus more material could be stored in this form.

Third, the codex was easier to hold and thus eliminated the cumbersome rolling and unrolling of the scroll. Finding a passage on a scroll would be like locating a sentence on a cassette tape by winding and rewinding until you found it. The codex made finding Scripture references much more convenient than fumbling around with a scroll. Most important for Christians, it allowed easy cross-reference from one section of the codex to another. One could move from Old to New Testament or from one book to another simply by sticking a finger or bookmark into the codex.

Since papyrus was not very suitable for books that were used frequently, within a few centuries Christians had switched to the more durable parchment — animal skins that had been specially treated to receive writing and cut into suitable size for pages. Since parchment was often expensive and hard to obtain, sometimes it would be erased by scraping and then used again. A manuscript written on reused parchment is called a "palimpsest." More than fifty of our biblical manuscripts dating from the fourth to the tenth centuries are palimpsests. Using ultraviolet or infrared light, modern researchers can detect the older, underlying text that can often provide important clues for textual research.

Exactly when the transition was made from papyrus to parchment and from scroll to codex is not known. But the evidence suggests that by the fourth century Christians used parchment almost exclusively for biblical manuscripts — a practice that lasted for almost a thousand years until the advent of printing on paper. Although we possess many papyrus fragments and partial texts, the most important biblical manuscripts are written on parchment in the codex form.

Ancient and Medieval Translations

Christians always focused on using texts for worship and guidance rather than prizing them simply for their sacred character or literary style. Thus manuscripts were not only copied but sometimes translated.

The oldest Jewish texts were written in Hebrew and collected over several centuries. As Hebrew gave way to Aramaic and as Greek became the dominant language of the Mediterranean world after the conquests of Alexander the Great (d. 323 B.C.), so many Jews were living outside the Holy Land that it became necessary to translate their Scriptures from Hebrew into Greek.

This Greek translation, begun about 250 B.C. in Alexandria, Egypt, is called the Septuagint (Latin for "seventy," hence the common abbreviation of this by the Roman numerals LXX). According to a legend, seventy-two scholars (six chosen from each of the twelve Jewish tribes) translated it in seventy-two days. Today we know that the translation really took several decades to complete. Although we do not know how the seventy-two got shortened to seventy, this translation has been called the Septuagint since the first century.

PREPARING FOR YOUR JOURNEY

"Easy access to Sacred Scripture should be provided for all the Christian faithful. That is why the Church from the very beginning accepted as her own that very ancient Greek translation of the Old Testament which is called the Septuagint; and she has always given a place of honor to other Eastern translations and Latin ones, especially the Latin translation known as the Vulgate.

But since the word of God should be accessible at all times, the Church by her authority and with maternal concern sees to it that suitable and correct translations are made into different languages, especially from the original texts of the sacred books. And should the opportunity arise and the Church authorities approve, if these translations are produced in cooperation with the separated brethren as well, all Christians will be able to use them."

— *VATICAN COUNCIL II*
Dogmatic Constitution on Divine Revelation, #22

Since the earliest Christians were Jews, they relied on the Jewish Scriptures for their basic understanding of who God was and why God entered human history. But from the time of Paul, in the middle of the first century, the Christian Church became more and more Greek speaking. Because these Christians were ignorant of Hebrew or Aramaic, they relied on and adopted the Greek Septuagint as their Scriptures.

Soon the Christians began adding their own important sacred texts. Early Christian manuscripts were copied and circulated with amazing speed through the network of communities scattered throughout the Mediterranean world.

The narrative gospel form, which was first used by Mark about A.D. 70, was known well enough to be imitated and revised by Matthew and Luke within a decade or so of Mark's composition. The letters of Paul were collected and circulated, probably in a papyrus codex, so that by the end of the first century the author of Peter could refer to "all his letters" and associate them with "the other scriptures" (2 Peter 3:16).

Although Latin was the official language of government and law in the first-century Roman Empire, the common language for business and travel in the eastern Mediterranean was Greek. All of the New Testament books were originally written in the Koine ("common," or popular) Greek dialect used in the first-century Roman world.

Whatever collections of Jesus' original words might have been available in Aramaic were soon translated into Greek for evangelization purposes. The Christian community's missionary progress in the Greek-speaking cities of the first-century Roman Empire transformed the Church from its rural Jewish roots into a new type of urban religious community. This community had its own doctrines, worship, and moral codes, all of which were formulated and circulated in Greek.

After the conversion of the Roman emperor Constantine in A.D. 313, the Roman government for the first time recognized Christianity as a legal religion. In 331, inspired by his newfound zeal for Christianity, Constantine ordered and paid for fifty parchment copies of the Christian Scriptures for the churches in his new capital city, Constantinople.

Fifty years later, Pope Damasus, who desired that some order be brought to the variety of existing Latin translations, urged Jerome to undertake the laborious task of translating the Hebrew and Greek Scriptures into Latin. Jerome's translation, called the Vulgate (Latin for "crowd," identifying it as a popular translation for everyone), was the most commonly used translation for the more than one thousand years that Latin dominated the intellectual life of Western Christianity. This Latin supremacy lasted until the Renaissance rediscovery of many ancient Greek and Hebrew biblical manuscripts. Luther and other Protestant scholars began to make use of these manuscripts instead of simply relying on the Vulgate translation.

Although Protestant scholars were beginning to employ the Greek and Hebrew texts for their translations, the Catholic Church staunchly maintained the Vulgate as its primary translation. In 1546, the Catholic ecumenical Council of Trent decreed that "this ancient Vulgate version is to be regarded as the authentic translation in public readings, disputations, sermons, and expositions."

Since then, dependence on the Vulgate has gradually diminished because scholars have increasingly had many more ancient manuscripts at their disposal. They have also significantly increased their knowledge of ancient languages and their critical skills in examining ancient texts. Modern Catholic translators of the Bible now consult not only the Latin but also a wide variety of ancient sources in Hebrew, Aramaic, Syriac, Coptic, and Greek.

Over the centuries, as Christian missionaries penetrated farther into the pagan realms of Europe, translations of the Latin Vulgate into the vernacular languages multiplied. Tracing only the English translations, we find that within a century of the conversion of England (ca. 600), there appeared paraphrases and translations in the Anglo-Saxon language done by such scholars as Caedmon and Bede. The first full translation of the Bible into English was done by John Wycliffe and others between 1382 and 1384. This Wycliffe Bible remained the most popular English version for the next two centuries until it was replaced by the King James Version (1611).

English Translations: Protestant

Beginning with the Protestant Reformation of the sixteenth century, Bible translators began to rely less on the Vulgate and more on the newly rediscovered Greek and Hebrew manuscripts that were becoming more available through the new printing technology. Protestant translations included those by William Tyndale (1525 – 31), Miles Coverdale (1535); John Rogers's Great Bible (1539 – 41); the Geneva Bible (1560), which was produced by exiled English

MODERN CRITICAL SCHOLARSHIP AND
THE SEARCH FOR MEANING

Modern critical scholarship begins with the basic truth that all meaning is contextualized. To discover the meaning of a text, we must pay attention to its contexts. Thus various methods and approaches have been devised to understand these contexts.

- We must recognize that we do not have the original manuscript of any biblical book, only copies of copies. Therefore we need to examine all relevant manuscripts to determine which are the best readings from all the variants. To achieve these goals, we use **textual criticism**.

- We must recognize that the meaning of any text depends upon the author's original intention (the literal sense). Communication (function) requires that we understand the author's choice of genre (form) in order to convey the author's intended meaning (content) in the circumstances in which the author wrote (the historical situation). To achieve these goals, we use **literary criticism** and the **historical-critical method.**

- We must recognize that many of the biblical books are complex, particularly in regard to the history of their composition and the transmission of their message. Therefore we need to distinguish between the many sources used, and we need to recognize the editorial layers in each book. To achieve these goals, we use **source criticism.**

- We must recognize the complexity of the Gospels, especially in how they developed from oral traditions into written documents. Therefore we need to distinguish between the many sources used, and we need to understand the editorial work of each evangelist. To achieve these goals, we use **redaction criticism.**

HOW THE BIBLE CAME TO BE

Protestants during the Catholic reign of Mary Tudor; and the Bishops' Bible (1568), done by a team of scholars.

In 1611 the King James Version was published. Despite some initial criticisms about its scholarship and language, it was authorized as the official translation for reading in churches, hence its designation as the Authorized Version. Gradually it became the most popular, widely used, and influential translation in the English language. A modernization of its archaic language (*thee, thou, thine, begat,* and so forth) appeared as the New King James Version (NKJV) between 1979 and 1982.

In the 1870s British scholars began a revision of the King James translation according to the more sophisticated standards of modern critical textual scholarship and a more extensive knowledge of the ancient biblical languages. But the Revised Version (RV)(1881 – 85) and its American counterpart the American Standard Version (ASV) (1901) never gained enough popularity to dethrone the King James Version. An updated revision called the New American Standard Bible (NASB) was published between 1963 and 1970.

Under the auspices of the National Council of Churches in America, a thorough revision of the King James Version, called the Revised Standard Version (RSV), appeared after World War II. Relying on the critical progress of modern scholarship, it balanced the desire to remain faithful to the King James Version and yet to render the meaning in more modern English. The Revised Standard Version was itself redone in 1990 in a more gender-sensitive translation called the New Revised Standard Version (NRSV). In 1996 the popular paraphrase *The Living Bible* was completely redone by a team of evangelical scholars and called The New Living Translation (NLT).

Many other English translations are now available. Some have been done under the auspices of various Christian Church organizations: the New English Bible (NEB) (1961 – 70) and its subsequent revision as the Revised English Bible (REB) of the British Protestant churches; the conservative evangelical New International Version (NIV) (1973 – 78) sponsored by the New York Bible Society; and Today's English Version: The Good News Bible (TEV) from the American Bible Society. Others have been done by individual scholars, such as J. B. Phillips's popular New Testament in Modern English and The Bible: An American Translation (1931) by University of Chicago professors E. J. Goodspeed and J. M. Powis Smith (often referred to as the Chicago Bible).

English Translations: Catholic

Catholics have also recognized the need for an approved vernacular translation. However, since the Council of Trent had declared the Vulgate to be the official translation, any Catholic translation was to be based on it rather than on the Greek or Hebrew. The first modern Catholic translation, done by English Catholic exiles, was the Douay-Rheims Version (1582–1609). The name comes from the two locations where its Old and New Testaments were published. Although somewhat literal and given to Latinisms because of its fidelity to the Vulgate, it influenced the Protestant translators of the King James Version.

A century and a half later (1749-63) this version underwent a thorough revision at the hands of London bishop Richard Challoner to modernize its style. The Rheims-Challoner Version remained the standard Catholic translation for almost two hundred years.

The need for a translation adapted to the language of the twentieth century spurred the American Catholic bishops, working with the Confraternity of Christian Doctrine, to sponsor the Confraternity Revision (1941) of the Rheims-Challoner New Testament, which would be suitable for both study and worship. A revision of the Old Testament was also begun, but it was abandoned when Pope Pius XII's 1943 encyclical on Catholic biblical studies *(Divino Afflante Spiritu)* permitted biblical scholars to consult the original languages and not just the Latin for their translation.

After World War II, the American bishops commissioned a new and more contemporary translation of the Bible from its original languages called The New American Bible (NAB), which was published in 1970. Although its New Testament was not quite finished, it was put into service when Vatican

Council II permitted the celebration of Mass in English. In preparation for the proposed revision of the English Lectionary for Mass (the collection of readings for Mass and other celebrations), the New Testament was thoroughly revised in 1986 and the Psalms in 1991. Further revisions of the Old Testament are now in progress.

Besides this official translation, there are other English translations by individuals as well as groups of scholars. In England, Oxford classics scholar Monsignor Ronald Knox translated the Vulgate (although he acknowledged the original languages in his footnotes) to create the Knox Bible (1944–50). In America, the New Testament (1950–54) by J. A. Kleist and J. L. Lilly rendered the Greek New Testament in fresh and vigorous modern American English.

Another major English translation, the 1966 Jerusalem Bible (JB), was based on the modern French translation *La Sainte Bible* produced by Dominican biblical scholars working in Jerusalem. It contains extensive footnotes and acquaints the reader with textual variants in the ancient manuscripts. The English version was further revised, and its translation significantly improved in the 1985 New Jerusalem Bible (NJB).

Which Books Belong in the Canon?

The procedures that were followed centuries ago to determine which books would be included in the biblical canon are now shrouded in the mists of history. Although we have no historical documentation about the process, or clearly expressed reasons for the canonical decisions, we believe that the Holy Spirit was guiding the churches to recognize the writings that could be considered sacred.

We know that between A.D. 150 and 367 a general consensus was forming about the books that now comprise our Bible. But exactly what happened during those two centuries is mostly speculation. We lack the historical data to unravel precisely why these books were selected out of the many that we now know were available in those early Christian communities.

Certainly one factor in the establishing of a Christian canon was the separation of Christianity from its Judaic roots. After the Roman destruction of the Jerusalem temple in A.D. 70, Christians and Pharisaic Jews vied to establish their respective forms of Judaism as the best way to be Jews without a temple. As each group struggled to create its distinctive identity, the divisions between the groups widened and the controversies became more heated, as is evident from the anti-Jewish sentiments that appear in the Gospels.

Christianity, which had begun as a group of Jews who recognized Jesus of Nazareth as the Jewish messiah, was now no longer considered Jewish. As a separate and distinctive religion, it adopted the Jewish books of the Greek Septuagint and added its own Christian writings. The result was the Christian Bible.

Probably the first books collected were the letters of Paul, which were written in the fifth decade of the first century. As was the custom in the ancient world, communities probably began copying these letters very soon after Paul wrote them. Although the individual letters were written in response to particular situations, their importance for the explanation of Christian doctrine and guidance for Christian living made them as useful then as they remain today.

The first collection of Paul's letters was very likely an arrangement by length of seven books identified by the names of the seven churches to which the letters were written (Romans, 1 and 2 Corinthians, Galatians, Ephesians, Philippians, Colossians, 1 and 2 Thessalonians). We also see the seven churches as representative of the whole Church in the seven messages of Christ to the churches in the book of Revelation (chapters 1–3).

The next collection was the four Gospels, which were written in the last third of the first century. Three of these Gospels — Matthew, Mark, and Luke — are very similar in viewpoint and presentation. Since they can easily be lined up in columns and viewed "at one glance" (*synoptic* in Greek), they are often called the synoptic Gospels. Scholars realize that these books depend on one another, but they disagree on exactly what the relationship is. John's Gospel, although developed independently of the other three, probably owes its existence to some familiarity with the narrative form used in the synoptic Gospels.

The various other books and letters of the New Testament were also composed during the postapostolic period from about A.D. 70 to 120. Although many of the New Testament books were quoted by Christian writers in the early second century, there is no indication that anything like an official canon existed at that time.

There is, however, evidence of a general consensus regarding the four Gospels and the Pauline letters, with continuing dialogue on the inclusion of some of the other letters and the book of Revelation. Other Christian books such as the Didache, the Shepherd of Hermas, 1 and 2 Letters of Clement, and the Letter of Barnabas were often grouped with the canonical books but were never officially included.

Closing the Canon

The canon began to be stabilized in the middle of the second century in large part because of those who were trying to make drastic changes to it.

At the one extreme was the heretic Marcion, who tried to make the canon too limited. In his zeal for a distinctive Christianity, Marcion rejected the Old Testament because of its inadequate doctrine of a wrathful God and its emphasis on the Law. In its place, he emphasized the Christian God of love and the gospel message. From his examination of the

New Testament, Marcion concluded that only Paul had really comprehended what Christianity was all about. But as the great church historian Adolf von Harnack so perceptively noted, "In the second century only one Christian — Marcion — took the trouble to understand Paul; but he misunderstood him!"

Marcion set to work to salvage his version of the genuine Christian message. His Bible contained only the Gospel of Luke and ten letters of Paul (the nine to the seven churches and the personal letter to Philemon). But he purged even these books of their "Jewish errors." He chopped out about 40 percent of the Gospel of Luke that he considered too Jewish, including the first two chapters that tell of the birth of Jesus. He cut many sections out of Paul's letters for the same reason. Accepting Marcion's canon would have meant the Church's complete repudiation of its Jewish roots — a step that neither the Roman nor the other communities were willing to take.

On the other end of the spectrum, the Gnostics sought to include in the canon a wide variety of other books. Gnosticism was a form of religion in late antiquity that valued insight or knowledge related to special divine revelations. It fostered a negative attitude toward the world and human society and offered deliverance from the burdens of earthly existence through special knowledge. It also promoted a dualistic approach that contrasted the evil material world with a good spiritual world.

Through early Christian writings that attacked these attitudes and through the recent discovery of many ancient Gnostic manuscripts, we are aware today of the many non-canonical or apocryphal writings that were available in early Christianity and that differed significantly from our canonical books.

These apocryphal works include gospels, which were often attributed to various apostles (e.g., Peter, Thomas, Philip, James); acts of apostles (John, Peter, Paul, Andrew); letters (to the Laodiceans, 3 Corinthians) and apocalypses (Peter). Studying these works can contribute to our historical knowledge of early Christianity and shed light on the formation and interpretation of our canonical books. But they remain of scholarly interest only and are not practical guides of our Christian lives.

There seem to have been several criteria for distinguishing authentic Christian writings: apostolic origin, the importance of the audience to which the writing was addressed, and usefulness for worship and church life. Books acquired a higher degree of trustworthiness and authority when they could be directly (as with the writings of Matthew, John, Peter, Paul) or indirectly (as with writings of Mark or Luke) traced to the teachings of an apostle. When their apostolic origin was questioned, as with Johannine authorship of the book of Revelation in the Eastern churches (about A.D. 250) or Pauline authorship of the letter to the Hebrews in the Western churches, their authority was diminished.

Books that were associated with major churches — for example, Mark (Rome), Luke and Matthew (Antioch), and John (Ephesus) — became widely distributed and consequently more influential. Others such as the letters of Philemon and Jude might have been more authoritative because of their recipients' important status within a Christian community.

The major factor, however, seems to have been the conformity of the content of these books with the general practice of the Christian life. These books were appropriate for reading during worship and suitable for prayer because they expressed genuine Christian beliefs, teachings, and moral guidelines.

By the end of the fourth century, the consensus on the canon was stabilizing. In his Easter letter of A.D. 367, Athanasius, bishop of Alexandria in Egypt, listed the twenty-seven books in our current New Testament, declaring that "in these alone is the teaching of true religion proclaimed as good news: let no one add to these or take anything from them."

That this canon became the standard is evident from both the Vulgate of Jerome (who was aware that the Latins did not accept the letter to the Hebrews and that the Greeks did not recognize the book of Revelation) and the official list of the Episcopal Council of Carthage (A.D. 397), which depended on a list from Hippo, where Augustine was bishop.

As I noted in the previous chapter, Protestants and Catholics at the time of the Reformation differed over which books belonged in the Old Testament. Following the stricter

Jewish tradition, Protestants accepted as canonical only the Old Testament books in Hebrew. Catholics, however, followed the wider Jewish tradition and so accepted as canonical the books from the Greek Septuagint (including the deutero-canonical books). Despite these differences, the Protestant churches made no changes in the New Testament canon.

Scholars are divided today about whether any newly discovered book could be accepted into the canon. Even if its apostolic origin and the importance of its original audience could be demonstrated, the fact that it has not been used by the Church for two millennia would probably disqualify it from receiving canonical status.

Questions for Reflection and Group Discussion

1. *Explain to a friend why there is no Greek manuscript that corresponds exactly to our modern translation of the New Testament.*
2. *How does the fact that the Bible is a collection of books make a difference to its reading and interpretation?*
3. *What are the advantages and disadvantages of reading a codex instead of a scroll? (To get a sense of how a scroll was read, take a roll of paper towels and pretend that the Gospel of Matthew is written on the inside.)*
4. *What are apocryphal gospels? Why would they not be included in our Bible?*

CHAPTER SEVEN

Biblical Authors and Audiences

An important result of serious Bible study is that we conquer our fear of "the Bible says" syndrome. So often we hear people claim "The Bible says . . ." as if simply stating what the Bible says were equivalent to explaining what the Bible means. Confusing *says* and *means* is the root of many difficulties in biblical interpretation.

The global claim that "the Bible says" is similar to "the government says" or "the Church says." What kind of authority would you give to someone who claimed that "the library says"? Wouldn't you want to know exactly where in the library the information came from?

The Bible is a collection of books that were written over a thousand-year period for audiences in diverse historical and cultural situations. For this reason we must move our compass beyond what "the Bible says" to a more precise awareness of who wrote what passage, for whom, in what circumstances, to convey what message, and for what reason. Without careful consideration of these issues, we cannot assume that what the words appear to say to us was what they meant to the original author who was inspired by God to write them.

The Catholic Church has wisely refrained from making any official doctrinal statement about the specific identity of any biblical author. In fact, we may never know for sure who most of the authors were. Determination of authorship depends on historical scholarship rather than belief. To question and investigate the authorship using modern historical scholarship in no way conflicts with our religious beliefs about the inspiration or canonicity of the biblical text.

Modern historical scholarship does not always agree with the traditional identifications of authors given by the early Church fathers, even though these might have been important for a book's inclusion in the canon. Accepting the canon that resulted from such judgments does not mean that we have to accept the ancient reasons for those judgments.

Authors in the Ancient World

In the ancient biblical world, perhaps only 10 percent of the population could read, and an even smaller percentage could write. Their societies functioned primarily through spoken words. Important words were memorized and passed down for generations without being written down. In an oral culture, what was not remembered was lost forever.

When we think of writing a book today, we picture the author sitting at a typewriter or computer and producing the whole text. For the ancients, writing was very often the last step in a long process of oral composition and transmission of stories, worship ceremonies, laws, proverbs, and other materials that had long been used by communities.

The Pentateuch as we have it, for example, was composed and edited over an eight-hundred-year period. It existed orally for centuries before being written down and carefully worked into its present canonical form from a variety of sources. Since the mid-nineteenth century, scholars have been trying to identify and reconstruct these sources.

The oral composition and transmission of community traditions modified and solidified them with each retelling. When the text was finally written down, the writer expressed his own creativity in how he collected and shaped the many traditional materials at his disposal. Authors were striving not for individual creativity but for accurate preservation of the traditions that guided the daily lives of their communities.

Who Wrote the Biblical Books?

Since most of the biblical books were rooted in oral traditions before they were written down, we have little knowledge about any of their composers. We learn about the identity and personality of the authors mostly through reflection on their writings. Some books, such as those by Old Testament prophets or New Testament evangelists and letter writers, show traces of the individual authors' interests and writing styles.

"A commentary attempts to interpret another man's words, to put into plain language what he expressed obscurely. Consequently, it gives the opinions of many people, and says: 'Some interpret the passage in this sense, some in that; these try to support their opinion and understanding of it by this evidence or reasoning: so that the wise reader, after reading these different explanations, and having familiarized himself with many that he can either approve or disapprove, may judge which is the best, and, like a good banker, may reject the money from a spurious mint.'"

— *ST. JEROME*
Apologia I.16

Paul certainly is the best-known writer of biblical books. Because his letters responded to specific problems in his ministry, they reveal much about Paul's personality. And although Jesus wrote no books, the Christian community cherished and carefully remembered his words after his death. His words are a mirror of his personality. They tip us off about his concerns, his hopes, his vision, and his values.

The biblical authors — the ones who actually wrote down the books as we have them — are mostly anonymous. But since manuscripts cannot just appear without someone writing them, credit for authorship was often given or attributed to others, in particular those figures whose stature in the community could give authority to the manuscript.

Thus Moses is the attributed author of the Pentateuch (the Torah, or Law), even though we know that these books underwent extensive editing for centuries after his death. David is the attributed author of the book of Psalms, even though many of them were composed by other people. Solomon is the attributed author of the Song of Songs and the book of Wisdom, even though the latter was composed in Greek some eight centuries after Solomon's death!

The identity of many New Testament authors is not as specific as we might suppose. Although we have names for the evangelists, for example, historical scholars today are not as quick to identify them with biblical persons who have the same names.

Since Mark and Luke are mentioned as coworkers of Paul and since Matthew and John are among the twelve apostles, they have traditionally been identified as the evangelists in order to reinforce the authority of their writings. But their texts offer few clues about them. They hide behind their texts just as modern novelists do. The message, not the author, is what they would want us to consider as most important.

Why Were the Biblical Books Written?

Since our Bible incorporates both the Jewish and Christian sacred books, we know that its original audience was made up of two distinct religious communities. As these communities developed, their needs changed. The changing needs of a community always guide the production of books. Authors write to solve difficulties that confront their audiences. Knowing something about a community's changing needs helps us understand why the authors wrote what they did.

As we might expect, no author simply decided to write a book of the Bible. Authors respond to problems and needs of communities. Every community requires some expression of its basic beliefs, its moral guidelines, and its worship practices. The Bible consists of the accumulated responses to these needs. All of the biblical books serve to form the faith community and maintain it. The various parts of the Old and New Testaments originated to help the community understand its identity and its relationship with God.

The Pentateuch is a narrative account of the nation of Israel becoming God's covenant partner. It recounts how the covenant was initiated by God through Abraham and established through Moses. It also specifies the requirements of the community for living in this relationship — hence its designation as Torah or instruction.

The historical books tell the ups and downs of the Israelite community as it struggled to live as God's people.

This endeavor began when Israel was but a loose confederation of tribes, and it continued through the confederation's development into a tightly controlled kingdom under the authority of a human king. The struggle took on yet another face when Israel was overthrown and colonized by other powerful empires. These national histories create a sense of identity for the community, encourage patriotic resistance when necessary, and offer examples of behavior that distinguish the community from other peoples surrounding it.

The prophetic books originated when the guidance of the king led the people away from God. In a world that did not clearly separate issues of religion and politics, church and state, prophets spoke out for God's ways. When social and political crises confronted their nation, prophets were lobbyists for following God's agenda rather than the royal one.

The wisdom books maintained and sustained the community's distinctive lifestyle with psalms for the various community liturgies, proverbs for instruction, and guidelines for the practice of everyday living. The mastery of everyday life is directly related to the mystery of God's creation. Careful and sober reflection yields a life worth living.

"I notice that your questions, which are all on the Gospels and the Epistles, show either that you do not read the Old Testament enough, or you do not understand it well enough, for it is involved in so many obscurities and types of future things that it all needs explanation."

— ST. JEROME
Letter 121

BIBLICAL AUTHORS AND AUDIENCES

The Gospels are the community-forming documents for Christians. They provide the guidelines for the Christian way of following Jesus and the blueprints for building Jesus' kingdom community here on earth. The gospel life of Jesus shows us the gospel life that every Christian is called upon to live.

The New Testament letters were written to clarify and address difficulties that arose for the early, developing faith communities. Missionaries such as Paul founded communities, stayed with them for a while, and then moved on to found new communities. Lacking any long-term training in their Christian beliefs and practices, early Christians were forced to make choices for which they were ill prepared. Often the result was conflict within the communities. Rather than let these conflicts fester, leaders used letters to help Christians understand their distinctive beliefs so that they could know what to practice. Sound Christian beliefs were still the basis for better Christian behavior.

The book of Revelation, which we find strange and puzzling, relates four revelatory visions that describe Christ at the center of the Church, the universe, the history of God saving humanity from evil, and the final divine transformation of our world. These visions encouraged the Christian community of that time to remain firm and endure the hostility of the Roman imperial government. The God who changed history by ripping the Jewish people from the oppression of the Egyptian Empire could not be far away from the oppressed

Christian community that, centuries later, needed to be
snatched from the grasp of the Roman Empire.

The Significance of Literary Forms

As readers, we learn to adjust our reading to whatever type
of writing we encounter. Each type creates expectations that
guide our reading. When we read our newspaper, we continually shift our reading as we scan the general news, sports,
comics, entertainment, and financial pages. We would also
apply different reading skills to a biography of Abraham
Lincoln, a history of Lincoln and the Civil War, or the poetry
of Walt Whitman that expresses his feelings about Lincoln's
death.

Each literary form requires different skills in order to
read it. Attentive readers recognize different types of writing
and adjust to these demands. They engage the appropriate
reading skills in order to discover the meanings the authors
have put into the text. By including many types of writing,
the Bible demands that we recognize what each form requires
and then shift gears to discern its meaning. Sorting out the
different types of literature is generally not a difficult task.

When examining a biblical book for its literary form,
we must first determine whether it is poetry or prose. Our
modern Bibles help us recognize these literary forms not
only by providing information in the introductions but also
by arranging the poetry into the characteristic ancient form

HOW THIS GUIDES INTERPRETATION

The goal of Scripture study is the discovery of *meaning* (moving beyond simple facts to determine their significance), which demands attention to the form, function, and content of the text.

The first step recognizes the *literary context.* We must learn to read the texts according to the demands of its literary form or genre. Determining what kind of literary form has been chosen by the author is essential.

The second step recognizes the *historical context.* The author's intended meaning (the literal sense) is known from the specific historical situation in which the text was composed.

The third step recognizes the *social, cultural and rhetorical*

Dogmatic Constitution on Divine Revelation, #12

However, since God speaks in Sacred Scripture through men in human fashion, the interpreter of sacred Scripture, in order to see clearly what God wanted to communicate to us, should carefully investigate what meaning the sacred writers really intended, and what God wanted to manifest by means of their words.

Those who search out the intention of the sacred writers must, among other things, have regard for the "literary forms." For truth is proposed and expressed in a variety of ways, depending on whether a text is history of one kind or another, or whether its form is that of prophecy, poetry, or some other type of speech.

The interpreter must investigate what the sacred writer intended to express and actually expressed in particular circumstances as he used contemporary literary forms in accordance with the situation of his own time and culture.

For the correct understanding of what the sacred author wanted to assert, due attention must be paid to the customary and characteristic styles of perceiving, speaking, and narrating which prevailed at the time of the sacred writer, and to the customs people normally followed at that period in their everyday dealings with one another.

But, since holy Scripture must be read and interpreted according to the same Spirit by whom it was written, no less serious attention must be given to the content and unity of the whole of Scripture, if the meaning of the sacred texts is to be correctly brought to light. The living tradition of the whole Church must be taken into account along with the harmony which exists between elements of the faith. It is the task of exegetes to work according to these rules toward a better understanding and explanation of the meaning of Sacred Scripture, so that through preparatory study the judgment of the Church may mature. For all of what has been said about the way of interpreting Scripture is subject finally to the judgment of the Church, which carries out the divine commission and ministry of guarding and interpreting the word of God.

context. We must know about the cultural situation in which the texts originated and how they function as a response to the needs of the original audience.

The understanding of the theological content of Scripture requires attention to the whole context of Scripture— to the living tradition in which it has been received, understood, and formulated, and to the connection that it has with other doctrinal formulations. Understanding the meaning of biblical truths requires that all these elements be examined. This interpretation is done under the guidance of the Church's teaching office in order that the Church's understanding of God through Scripture might develop to its fullness.

of balanced couplets rather than in regular paragraphs. Although poetry and prose both aim to influence the audience, the function of specific types of writing varies. Some books are meant to entertain, others to educate or inform, and others to edify by providing encouragement or examples to follow.

"Once readers have determined the literary form of any biblical book or passage, standards applicable to that form help to clarify what the author meant, i.e., the literal sense. . . . Many past difficulties about the Bible have stemmed from the failure to recognize the diversity of literary forms that it contains and from the tendency to misinterpret as scientific history pieces of the Bible that are not historical or are historical only in a more popular sense. . . . If one correctly classifies a certain part of the Bible as fiction, one is not destroying the historicity of that section, for it never was history; one is simply recognizing the author's intention in writing that section. . . . Biblical fiction is just as inspired as biblical history."

— *REV. RAYMOND E. BROWN, S.S.*
New Jerome Biblical Commentary, "Hermeneutics," # 71:25 – 26

Poetry especially characterizes the psalms, which are songs for celebration; the prophetic oracles, especially those that report what God speaks; the proverbs and wisdom instructions, which needed to be memorized for practical living; and the prayers said by both individuals and groups.

Prose characterizes the narrative materials, which include the Pentateuch, the historical books, the Gospels, and the Acts of the Apostles. The New Testament letters, which

PREPARING FOR YOUR JOURNEY

clarify doctrines and offer encouragement for Christian living, are also in prose form.

This variety of literary types and styles of expression in the biblical books reminds us that the Bible is a library rather than a single book. Moreover, as the community's book, it contains the treasured memories of how the community began, how it changed over time, and how it lives out its call to be the people of God. Anyone entering into this community today needs to be aware of these family memories. Our choice of these particular books as those that orient our life in the Christian community makes them permanently relevant.

Questions for Reflection and Group Discussion

1. *Give an example of the difference between what someone says and what that person means.*
2. *How would our explanation of the divine inspiration of biblical texts be affected by our knowledge that some biblical texts were composed orally and used for decades or centuries before being written down?*
3. *What is the relationship between the identity of the author and the truth of the text?*
4. *Does the fact that many authors of biblical books are unknown bother you? Why or why not?*
5. *What difference does it make if we know that some biblical books are attributed to people who did not write them?*

BIBLICAL AUTHORS AND AUDIENCES

CHAPTER EIGHT

A Bible Explorer's Travel Kit

Whenever we go on a journey, the kind of trip and how long we will be gone determine what kind of luggage we will need. If it's an overnight trip, we can just take a small bag. For a weekend, a small suitcase will do. And for a very long trip we might need several bags or a trunk.

Whenever we pack for a trip, we decide what is essential and what we would like to take if we have room or if we have a special need. Since we cannot pack everything for our Bible journey, we have to ask ourselves two questions: What are the essentials? and What are the extra things we can choose, depending on our special interests?

There are two essentials: a good translation and a Bible dictionary. The other helps I will mention are things you can acquire only if you are interested.

The First Essential: A Good Translation

The first requirement for our journey is a good translation of the Bible. Bible translations come in a dizzying variety not only of bindings, sizes, and costs but also of styles of translation. Some try to be very exact, while others paraphrase the authors' meaning rather than the exact words. Some digest certain passages and eliminate others. Many Bibles provide helpful notes to aid the reader, while others have no notes at all. And in our computer age, most of the Bible translations and many of the Bible helps I will mention are now available on CD-ROM or on-line services for personal or office computers.

Bibles are most easily identified by the name of their translation. When you go to a bookstore to purchase a Bible or wish to invest in one for your computer, you need to ask for the specific translation you want, because the same translation can be marketed by many different publishers.

First, a word of caution. The older standard Bibles like the Catholic Douay-Rheims Version and the Protestant King James Version have such archaic language that they are unsuitable for reading today. They have been surpassed by many more excellent modern translations. But they still retain important historical interest because of their influence both on the English language and on all subsequent English translations. Since the King James was the most widely used and probably the most commonly read book in the English language

PREPARING FOR YOUR JOURNEY

until this century, its phrases resonate throughout English literature, and many biblical allusions are still recognized in their familiar King James form.

Despite several attempts to bring the King James Version up to date in the American Standard Version, the Revised Standard Version, the New American Standard Bible, and the New King James Version, these revisions all suffer from the same problems. Scholars today have more and better ancient manuscripts than were available to the earlier translators. They also have a more sophisticated understanding of the ancient biblical languages. Moreover, the English language has changed — and is constantly changing — from its seventeenth century form. These changes need to be recognized and incorporated into any translation for a modern audience.

There are many modern Bible translations to choose from. As you read the Bible more and more, you might wish to compare some of these translations to discover new riches. Since no translation from one language to another fully communicates all that the original does, every translation has positive and negative features.

The first two translations in the following list are the best Catholic translations available. Catholic Bibles have normally included many helps in the form of footnotes for the reader. Protestant Bibles have tended to omit all notes except a few that informed readers about important manuscript variations that could lead to different possible translations of a particular verse. Now, however, almost all translations have an annotated edition that includes helpful resources for readers. When purchasing any translation, always look for the annotated edition.

"Lord, who can comprehend even one of your words? We lose more of it than we grasp, like those who drink from a living spring. For God's word offers different facets according to the capacity of the listener, and the Lord has portrayed the message in many colors, so that whoever gazes on it can see in it what is suitable. Within it God has buried manifold treasures, so that each of us might grow rich in seeking them out."

— *ST. EPHRAEM*
Commentary on the Diatessaron

The **New American Bible** (NAB) is the finest Catholic translation available in American English. Done by members of the Catholic Biblical Association of America under the sponsorship of the U.S. bishops, it is the first American Catholic translation that is not based entirely on the Latin Vulgate. Instead, the translators used the original Hebrew and Greek texts, with a critical use of all ancient sources (including the Latin). This translation is used for the Bible readings chosen to be read at Sunday Mass. It contains brief introductions to each book as well as cross-references to other biblical passages. The excellent footnotes provide immediate help for readers who can be puzzled by what they

PREPARING FOR YOUR JOURNEY

read. In the revisions some attempt has been made to use more gender-sensitive inclusive language for humans but not for God.

The **New Jerusalem Bible** (NJB) is another outstanding Catholic version. When the Jerusalem Bible was first translated into English in 1966, it relied primarily on the French translation done by scholars at the Dominican Biblical School in Jerusalem. The revision (1985) pays much more attention to the original biblical languages. Besides having excellent introductions, its outstanding feature is its extensive notes that were also updated for the revision. Since the translation was done primarily by British scholars, sometimes the English is more British than American. You should be careful not to get the Reader's Edition, which does not contain the notes.

You should also consider the following translations. Although they are not specifically Catholic, Catholic Scripture scholars have participated on the translation committees of some of these. If you decide to purchase one, ask for a version that includes the Catholic deuterocanonical books, or the Protestant Apocrypha, which are not always found in Protestant Bibles. Most of these translations have an edition that includes these deuterocanonical books.

The following descriptions are based in part on each version's own introduction and explanatory notes. Any quoted material is from those introductions.

The **Revised Standard Version** (RSV), although a revision of the King James, is still a helpful translation because of its accuracy. It strives to preserve the Greek and Hebrew sentence structure and word order when possible. One scholar claimed that if every Greek manuscript of the New Testament were somehow destroyed, we could re-create the Greek text from the RSV. The accuracy of this translation can be a fine complement or counterbalance to translations that are not so literal.

"We do not look upon the Bible as an authority for science or history. We see truth in the Bible as not to be reduced solely to literal truth, but also to include salvation truths expressed in varied literary forms."

— *U.S. BISHOPS*
"A Pastoral Statement for Catholics on Biblical Fundamentalism" (1987)

The **New Revised Standard Version** (NRSV) is a thorough revision of the RSV that introduces changes "warranted on the basis of accuracy, clarity, euphony, and current English usage." This translation is distinctive for the care it has taken to eliminate masculine-oriented language relating to people (not God) insofar as could be done without distorting passages that reflect the historical situation of ancient patriarchal culture and society. Its guiding maxim is to achieve a translation that is "as literal as possible, as free as necessary." This translation is used for study and worship by Catholic churches in Canada and by many mainline Protestant churches.

The **New International Version** (NIV) is a multipurpose translation by evangelical scholars from several English-speaking nations. They wanted a translation that would be accurate without being literal, and suitable for "public and private reading, teaching, preaching, memorizing and liturgical use." They achieved a continuity with the older, more familiar style of biblical language in a form that was more readable because they eliminated archaic words, modified sentence structure, and were generally sensitive to the contextual meaning and connotations of words.

The **Good News Bible: Today's English Version** (TEV) is an attempt to put the Bible into language that everyday people can read instead of the more formal biblical language we usually hear. Through close examination of the ancient texts, the translators wanted to reproduce for the modern reader the meanings of the original without resorting to traditional biblical vocabulary or style. Their work did much to promote the method of translation that strives for dynamic equivalence, that is, a thought-for-thought translation instead of the word-for-word style of translation that had been used for the traditional English translations.

The **Revised English Bible** (REB) began as a project of the Church of Scotland in 1946 but soon developed into a joint effort with most of the non-Catholic churches of Great Britain. In 1970, their translation was published as the New English Bible (NEB). In 1989, a thorough revision appeared as the Revised English Bible (REB). Like other translations that were moving away from the idea that translations should reproduce the word order and sentence structure of the original, the NEB adopted the dynamic-equivalence method. Their goal was "understanding the original as precisely as we could (using all available aids), and then saying again in our own native idiom what we believed the author to be saying in his." They achieved a fresh literary style (more British than American) that is also very suitable for oral reading in worship.

The **New Living Translation** (NLT) attempts to resolve a difficult issue. One of the most popular English versions

---

THE THREE STEPS
IN TRANSLATING THE BIBLE

Translating the Bible is the result of many choices, both textual and linguistic (verbal and grammatical).

1. *Determine the text.* Since no original manuscripts of any biblical books exist, scholars examine and compare all the various manuscripts to determine as accurately as possible which text ought to be translated. There is no ancient manuscript that corresponds exactly to the Bible we now have.

2. *Determine the meaning in the original language.* Disagreements arise concerning the meaning of individual words in various literary, cultural, and doctrinal contexts.

3. *Determine the meaning in the receptor language.* Disagreements occur concerning which words best capture the shades of meaning found in the original. How one attempts to bridge the

---

PREPARING FOR YOUR JOURNEY

of the Bible, with over forty million copies sold, is *The Living Bible* by Kenneth Taylor. This is not a real translation but a paraphrase. As Taylor admits in his preface, it is "a restatement of the author's thoughts, using different words than he did." The positive value of paraphrasing is that it can help one understand the meaning of difficult passages. The danger, as Taylor himself also notes, is that "whenever the author's exact words are not translated from the original languages, there is a possibility that the translator, however honest, may be

---

gap between the two languages depends on one's theory of translation.

- A **literal translation** focuses on the form of the original and follows as closely as possible the words of the original as long as they can be understood in the receptor language. It strives to retain the historical distance of the two languages at all times.

- A **free translation** (paraphrase) focuses on the ideas rather than the words of the original. It strives to eliminate all historical distance between the original and the receptor languages.

- A **dynamic-equivalent translation** attempts to express the original meaning in appropriately modern form without eliminating the historical distance between the two languages.

giving the English reader something that the original writer did not mean to say."

The success of *The Living Bible* prompted a group of ninety evangelical scholars to remedy the dangers associated with its paraphrasing. They carefully compared the text of *The Living Bible* to the original Greek and Hebrew texts and in 1996 published the general-purpose translation called The New Living Translation (NLT), which attempts to combine easy readability with accuracy for study.

How to examine a translation

When comparing translations, the most important information is usually found in the introduction. The introduction provides clues about why the translators thought there should be one more translation even though dozens are now available. Most important, it also sheds light on the principles that guided their work as translators. A Bible's introduction and table of contents should answer several basic questions.

Which books does it include? Does it include the deuterocanonical or apocryphal books that the Catholic Church accepts in its canon? Whether it has these books can be an important consideration because without them, you will be unable to find biblical books and readings that Catholics refer to and use at Mass. If a Catholic version is available, it will probably incorporate the deuterocanonical books into their usual place in the Catholic order. If they are included only in a special section at the end of the Bible, you will need to read the introduction to that section to discover how to find what you are looking for.

Which manuscripts does it depend on?   Does it rely on the best available Hebrew, Aramaic, and Greek manuscripts, or does some particular translation (whether ancient or modern) govern its work? Some Bibles are revisions of previous translations, such as the King James, and merely seek to modernize the language. Others, such as the Jerusalem Bible, which was based on the French *La Sainte Bible,* are translations of translations rather than of the ancient texts.

Which theory of translation does it use?   Translating the Bible has become more and more sophisticated. Although every translation attempts to convey the meaning of the ancient Hebrew and Greek texts as accurately as possible to the modern reader, there are generally two schools of thought about how to do it.

The more literal approach seeks a "formal equivalence" between the words of the original language and the corresponding words of the modern language. This word-for-word emphasis seeks to keep as much as possible the word order and sentence structure of the ancient languages. Its overriding concern is accuracy and fidelity to the *author's words.*

The other approach seeks a "dynamic equivalence" between the message of the original language and its counterpart in the modern language. This thought-for-thought emphasis also seeks to create as much as possible the same impact on modern readers that the original had on its audience. Its overriding concern is idiomatic power and fidelity to the *author's thoughts*.

Parallel Bibles

For easy comparison of different translations, there are parallel Bibles that include several versions side by side on each page. Unfortunately, due to space considerations, they omit the scholarly notes that are found in the NAB and the NJB.

The **Complete Parallel Bible** from Oxford University Press includes four translations — the New American Bible (NAB), the New Jerusalem Bible (NJB), the New Revised Standard Version (NRSV), and the Revised English Bible (REB) — arranged in columns so that the corresponding verses appear on each page. As you might expect, this is a very fat book, and it is not easy to hold in your hands to read. But it does give you immediate access to the complete text of four important modern versions.

The **Layman's Parallel Bible** from Zondervan features the KJV, the NIV, the NRSV, and *The Living Bible*. This allows the reader to inspect the various styles of translation, from the word-for-word KJV and its most recent revision, the NRSV,

One way to get a sense of the different versions that result from the two basic methods of translation is simply to list the different types that exemplify the spectrum of translation styles.

Very literal, but not very readable:
- King James Version
- New King James Version
- New American Standard Bible

Accurate and readable
(formal equivalent — word-for-word emphasis):
- Revised Standard Version
- New American Bible
- New Revised Standard Version

Accurate and readable
(dynamic equivalent — thought-for-thought emphasis):
- New Jerusalem Bible
- New International Version
- The Good News Bible: Today's English Version
- Revised English Bible

Very readable, but not very literal:
- New Living Translation
- The Message

Paraphrase:
- The Living Bible

to the thought-for-thought NIV and the paraphrased *The Living Bible.*

The **Precise Parallel New Testament,** also from Oxford, includes eight translations — the United Bible Societies' Greek text (fourth edition), the KJV, the Rheims New Testament, the Amplified Bible, the NIV, the NRSV, the NAB, and the NASB. These translations allow you to consider the original Greek, the great historic English texts, and several modern translations that exemplify the different methods of translation that distinguish Bibles today.

Which translation is best?

Probably the most commonly asked question of Bible seekers is, Which Bible translation is best? The answer hinges on why you want to use the Bible. Bibles can be read for a variety of reasons — for personal reading, for study, for private prayer, or for public reading during community worship. Your reasons for reading the Bible can help you to determine which translation you might find most suitable.

Remember that since languages never correspond directly with one another, every translation is to some extent an interpretation of the Bible's meaning. Readers should compare one or more translations to recognize the different ways scholars have attempted to express the original meaning of the Bible in a modern way. You might find it helpful to compare one or two Bibles to determine which one you prefer.

For personal reading use a translation that is readable and accessible. Beginning to read the Bible can be a challenge. Using a translation that tries to make the reading easier is often a good way to start. Bibles that are guided by the philosophy of dynamic equivalence (thought-for-thought translation) are in general more suitable for personal reading. By using such popular translations as the New Jerusalem Bible, the New International Version, the New Living Translation, the Good News Bible: Today's English Version, or the Revised English Bible, you will gain an introduction to the story and the message of the Bible in language that strives to make the text reader friendly.

Often for our personal reading we want to experience the biblical text in a way that grabs us or speaks to us in language that is familiar to us. Several modern translations have attempted to give the reader a feel for the everyday style of the Greek in which the original New Testament texts were written. One modern attempt to do this is the New Testament translation by Eugene Peterson called *The Message* from NavPress.

Peterson's language is earthy and forceful. He helps us sense the impact that the text might have made on its first listeners. But the danger in converting "the tone, the rhythm, the events, the ideas, into the way we actually think and speak" is that we no longer get the words that the original writers wrote. Reading Peterson is a treat, but it is best done in conjunction with a translation that strives for accuracy.

For Bible study use a translation that is reliable and accurate. The best Bible for study is one that gives accuracy

in translation and provides scholarly notes to help with difficult passages. The New American Bible and the New Revised
Standard Version, which put more emphasis on the formal-
equivalence theory of translation, are most helpful for careful
study because they focus on the author's own words.

"In the Holy Scriptures you can make no progress unless you have a
guide to show you the way."

— *ST. JEROME*
Letter 53

They also allow the reader to get a flavor of the grammatical syntax and sentence structure of the original. Since
they strive to represent as accurately as possible what the
author said, they can convey the obscurity and the often awk-
ward or complicated expression of the original. Where the
original text is unclear, as in several sections of Paul's letters,
this can be illustrated and not simply glossed over by presenting what someone thinks the author was trying to say.

Study Bibles

To respond to the growing interest in Bible study, many publishers have created special editions of the Bible that include
many of the helps that beginners need. If you are going to
purchase a new Bible, you might consider one of these study
Bibles as a way to get both a modern translation and some

convenient study helps. Most study Bibles include maps, extensive notes and application helps, historical and literary background, and a glossary or brief dictionary of important terms.

A very good investment for the serious seeker would be one of the two excellent study Bibles published by Oxford University Press, the **Catholic Study Bible** or the **Catholic Bible: Personal Study Edition** (1995). These include the whole NAB translation as well as background articles and helpful reading guides for every book of the Bible. Although it costs a bit more, you should consider the hardbound edition, which will last longer despite abundant use. The **HarperCollins Study Bible** includes the NRSV translation and excellent notes done by an ecumenical group of biblical scholars that included several Catholics. There are numerous study Bibles that use the NIV translation.

The Second Essential: A Bible Dictionary

Just as a tour guide tells you about the background and history of the places you visit, so a Bible dictionary or encyclopedia supplies material about the people, places, things, and themes that you encounter in your reading. The best single-volume ones to examine are *Harper's Bible Dictionary, Oxford Dictionary of the Bible, The Mercer Dictionary of the Bible, Eerdmans Handbook to the Bible,* and John L. McKenzie's *Dictionary of the Bible,* which although now somewhat dated, relates the biblical information to Catholic theology and doctrine. There are also several multivolume resources such as the five-volume *Interpreter's Dictionary of the Bible* and the six-volume *Anchor Bible Dictionary*, which is the finest and most up-to-date multivolume encyclopedia available. It is also obtainable on CD-ROM for your home computer through Logos Research Systems.

A slightly different dictionary that is of great interest for anyone wanting to apply the discoveries of their biblical study to ministry is the *Collegeville Pastoral Dictionary of Biblical Theology*, edited by the late Fr. Carroll Stuhlmueller and members of the faculty at Catholic Theological Union in Chicago. The articles not only present the best results of modern critical biblical scholarship but also relate them to the pastoral-liturgical tradition of the Church.

Optional Helps

There are numerous other helps that can make your Bible reading journey more rewarding. These resources are the foundation for your home Bible reference library. Although these are not essential, they supply the background that can make your reading journey richer and more enjoyable. Before purchasing any, you might want to take time to browse through your local bookstore or public library, or better yet in a seminary or academic (college or university) library or a Catholic bookstore, to examine them for yourself.

Commentaries

For working your way through the individual books of Scripture, your best help is a commentary. Commentaries, which discuss the meanings of the biblical text, come in various degrees of difficulty.

Beginning commentaries take you through larger units of the text so that you get the general flavor of the biblical book. They provide enough detail to enhance your reading but not so much that you bog down. Perhaps the finest Catholic commentary on this level is the *Collegeville Bible Commentary.* Covering every book of the Bible, these come individually in a handy pamphlet size and include the NAB text on the top part of the page and the running commentary below. Study questions are also included. The complete commentary, without the Bible text, is also published in separate Old and New Testament volumes or in a convenient single-volume edition.

Intermediate-level commentaries add more detailed information and cover the biblical text almost verse by verse. Examples of this type include the several volumes in the as-yet-incomplete *Sacra Pagina* series from Glazier-Liturgical Press, the *Interpretation Bible Study* commentaries for teaching and preaching from Westminster / John Knox Press, the twelve-volume *New Interpreter's Bible,* and the several *Abingdon New Testament Commentaries* from Abingdon Press. These commentaries are readable and yet challenging because they reveal the depths of meaning that the biblical texts can conceal.

Advanced commentaries are the type that scholars use. They deal with the biblical books in great detail and often contain far more information than we ever imagined. However, you can often read these with great profit when you wish to explore specific chapters or verses or particularly puzzling passages in greater depth. Perhaps the best place to locate these is in a seminary or university library.

There are also one-volume Bible commentaries that contain explanations for each biblical book. Examples include *Harper's Bible Commentary, The International Bible Commentary, The Interpreter's One-Volume Commentary on the Bible, The NIV Bible Companion,* and *The Women's Bible Commentary.*

"For there are some secret places in the Holy Scriptures into which God has not wished us to penetrate more deeply and, if we try to do so, the deeper we go, the darker and darker it becomes, so we are thus led to recognize the unsearchable majesty of the divine wisdom, and the weakness of the human mind."

— *ERASMUS*
On Free Will, Preface

The finest Catholic one-volume Bible commentary is *The New Jerome Biblical Commentary* (1990), edited by Fr. Raymond Brown, Fr. Joseph Fitzmyer, and Fr. Roland

Murphy. Besides thorough introductions and detailed commentary for each biblical book, this volume contains more than twenty topical articles covering the basic material that any seeker would want to know about the Bible. If there were only one book to put in your home reference library, this would be it. An abbreviated and somewhat simplified version of this, called *The New Jerome Bible Handbook,* is published by the Liturgical Press. This digest contains only very brief introductory material and no detailed comment on the biblical books.

Atlases of the Bible

An atlas of biblical lands, with historical and geographical maps, is helpful for situating the Bible in its physical environment. There are many to choose from. The *Hammond Atlas of the Bible* is inexpensive and yet contains excellent maps. Others to look at include *The Macmillan Bible Atlas, The Harper Atlas of the Bible,* and the *Oxford Bible Atlas.* Many Bible computer programs also include maps.

Synopses of the four Gospels

As you begin to study the Gospels more thoroughly, you might wish to purchase a synopsis, which places the texts side by side in order to detect more easily the differences between the individual Gospels. This allows you to study the unique contributions of each evangelist, as scholars do in what they call redaction (editing) criticism. Burton Throckmorton's *Gospel Parallels* is a synopsis of the first three Gospels. Its older edition used the RSV translation, and a revised edition uses the newer NRSV text. *A Synopsis of the Four Gospels,* edited by Kurt Aland, is available from the American Bible Society.

Bible concordances

Another handy tool is a concordance, an alphabetical list of the principal words in the Bible along with citations of their locations and a brief portion of the sentence in which each is used. This makes tracing themes or finding passages more convenient. Since different Bibles might translate the same original word differently in English, a concordance must be correlated to the specific translation you are using. Although concordances still come in printed volumes, having a Bible translation on your computer gives you a faster and better concordance because most programs allow you to search the text not only for single words but also for particular phrases or combinations of words.

Questions for Reflection and Group Discussion

1. *Which Bible translation do you have? If other members of your discussion group have different translations, compare some verses to see how they differ.*

2. *What is the difference between a dynamic-equivalent and a formal-equivalent translation? If members of the group have different translations, determine which category each belongs to.*

3. *What is a concordance? Why does it have to be correlated to a particular translation?*

4. *Explain the difference between a commentary on John's Gospel and a book about it.*

PART THREE

Making Your Journey

Continue your search for truth. *Recall the words of one of your great friends, St. Augustine: "Let us seek with the desire to find, and find with the desire to seek still more." Happy are those who, while possessing the truth, search more earnestly for it in order to renew it, deepen it, and transmit it to others. Happy also are those who, not having found it, are working toward it with a sincere heart. May they seek the light of tomorrow with the light of today until they reach the fullness of light.*

But do not forget that if thinking is something great, it is first a duty. Woe to whoever voluntarily closes their eyes to the light. Thinking is also a responsibility, so woe to those who darken the spirit by the thousand tricks which degrade it, make it proud, deceive and deform it. What other basic principle is there for thinkers except to think rightly?

— *VATICAN II BISHOPS*
Closing message to scientists and thinkers (8 December 1965)

CHAPTER NINE

A Quick Tour
of the Bible

Whenever visiting a city for the first time, it is good to start
with one of those daylong tours that hits all the important
tourist sights. Your initial reading journey is like one of these
scenic tours. It provides a general acquaintance with the famous places that no tourist would want to miss. At the same
time, it whets your appetite for further excursions to these
places to explore them in greater detail.

As you take up your Bible to read, where should you
begin, and how should you work your way through it? You
could follow the trite wisdom of the King of Hearts in *Alice
in Wonderland,* who advises that you should "begin at the
beginning and go on til you come to the end: then stop."
However, since the Bible is a library of very different books,
you might not derive much pleasure or profit simply by

IMPORTANT DATES IN BIBLICAL HISTORY

Old Testament Era

ca. 1800 B.C. Abraham called, and covenant relationship begins

ca. 1250 Exodus of the Hebrews from Egypt, with Moses as their leader

ca. 1200 Conquest of Canaan and confederation of the twelve tribes

ca. 1000 David becomes king; Jerusalem chosen as capital

ca. 970–931 Solomon is king; first temple built in Jerusalem

ca. 930 Solomon's kingdom divided into Israel (north) and Judah (south)

ca. 850 Ministry of the prophet Elijah

ca. 740 Call of First Isaiah; Assyrian expansion and domination

721 Fall of Samaria; end of northern kingdom

701 Assyrian king Sennacherib invades Judah, but Jerusalem is spared

621 King Josiah's reform (also called the deuteronomic reform)

612 Babylonian destruction of Assyrian capital Nineveh

598 First Babylonian capture of Jerusalem; exile of royalty

587 Babylonian destruction of first Jerusalem temple; exile of Jews

538 Decree of Cyrus the Great of Persia ends Jewish exile in Babylon

520 Preaching of prophets Haggai and Zechariah to rebuild temple

515 Dedication of the second temple, which was rebuilt after exile

ca. 450–400 Restoration by Ezra (priest) and Nehemiah (Persian governor)

ca. 400 Pentateuch completed (same as its present form)

333 – 23 Reign of Alexander the Great; Hellenistic world
domination
167 – 164 Maccabeean revolt against Greek Seleucid king
Antiochus IV
164 Desecrated temple is rededicated (Hanukkah)
63 Romans achieve world domination
37 Herod the Great becomes king of Judea
ca. 4 Jesus of Nazareth is born

New Testament Era

26 – 36 A.D. Pontius Pilate is Roman procurator in Judea
27 Beginning of the public ministry of Jesus
30 or 33 Crucifixion of Jesus in Jerusalem
ca. 36 Saul (Paul) of Tarsus converted to the Christian "Way"
46 – 49 Paul's first missionary journey
ca. 49 Apostolic meeting in Jerusalem opens community
to Gentiles
49 – 52 Paul's second missionary journey (letters begin ca. 50)
54 – 57 Paul's third missionary journey
58 – 63 Paul arrested; goes to Rome for trial
64 Emperor Nero burns Rome; Christians are blamed and
persecuted
ca. 67 Martyrdom of Peter and Paul under Nero; Apostolic
Age ends
70 Roman destruction of second Jerusalem temple (which
is never rebuilt)
73 Final defeat of Jewish rebels against Rome at fortress
of Masada
ca. 85 Pharisaic control of Judaism begins exclusion
of Christians
132 – 135 Romans end messianic revolt of Bar Kochba;
Christianity now independent of Judaism

A QUICK TOUR OF THE BIBLE

beginning with the first one on the shelf and reading straight through until you have read them all.

But if you do wish to read it straight through, your best companion is a good study Bible such as the *Oxford Catholic Study Bible.* Besides having the whole NAB translation and notes, it has almost six hundred pages of reading guides that lead you through the text. For each book, first read the introduction and then use as many of the study helps and notes as you can to understand the book's meaning. You might also wish to have a Bible dictionary or a one-volume commentary for further help.

Another approach would be to read what most interests you. For Christians, a good starting point is the Gospel of Luke and its companion volume, the Acts of the Apostles. They offer a basic summary of Jesus' life and ministry as well as the life and ministry of the early Church. This gives you a framework in which to understand the other New Testament books and to appreciate their contributions to the creation of a distinctively Christian way of life.

A Practical Travel Plan for Your Reading Journey

Instead of reading the Bible straight through or simply reading eclectically, a more practical and enjoyable approach is to read the biblical story in a way that re-creates the experience of the biblical community. This way you can follow the growth and development of the Jewish and Christian communities as they figure out how to live their relationship with God. This approach also reinforces your awareness of the historical chronology and of the changing circumstances in which the biblical books were written.

"It is the duty of good education to arrive at wisdom by means of a definite order."

— *ST. AUGUSTINE*
Soliloquies, 1:13:23

The plan of suggested readings that follows is one that I helped develop for the four-year adult Bible study course of the *Denver Catholic Biblical School Program,* published by Paulist Press. Following this travel plan also ensures that you will read every book of the Bible on your initial journey. The four *Student Workbooks* for this Bible study program contain specific questions suitable for either group discussion or individual study for each biblical book. Although this program was designed to work with the guidance of a trained teacher, you might find that these questions help you and your fellow travelers get more out of your reading journey.

Old Testament Foundations: From Exodus to Exile

A good place to begin your Bible reading is with the story of the covenant-making experience of the Hebrew people when they were delivered from oppression in Egypt (the books of

Exodus, Numbers, Leviticus, and Deuteronomy). This is the most important experience in the Old Testament, and it serves as the pattern or guideline for the Hebrews' entering into and maintaining their covenant relationship with God. In this experience, they learned for the first time who God was, what God wanted by breaking into their lives, and who they were in relation to God. This exodus experience is the key for unlocking the meaning of God's search for partnership with a human community. From this experience, the Jewish people could look back to their ancestral stories and their relationship to all humanity (the book of Genesis), and forward to the historical development of the people (the historical and prophetic books).

The Exodus

Exodus 1 – 6	The Call of Moses
Exodus 7 – 13	Plagues and Passover
Exodus 14 – 15	The exodus
Exodus 16 – 18	The desert
Exodus 19 – 24	The Sinai covenant and Moses' Torah
Exodus 25 – 31	The Ark of the Covenant
Exodus 24:12 – 18; 32 – 34	The golden calf
Leviticus 12 – 14, 16, 19, 23, 26	The covenant laws
Numbers 6, 9 – 14, 16, 17, 20 – 24	Forty years wandering to the Promised Land
Deuteronomy 1, 4 – 11	A new focus on the covenant
Deuteronomy 29 – 34	Moses' last sermon and death

The exodus story is found in the part of the Old Testament that the Jews call the Law, or Torah. But these books are not written like law books but as a story of the people's special covenant relationship with God. They describe the original experience of the Israelite community's relationship with God. Everything else in the Old Testament is, in one way or other, a working out of this essential experience.

The narrative begins with the book of Exodus, in which Moses is called to be the people's leader and the Hebrew people are liberated from oppression in Egypt. The story continues through Leviticus, in which their covenant and its obligations are described; Numbers, which recounts their wandering through the wilderness for forty years; and Deuteronomy, which tells of their arrival and entry into the Promised Land.

The story relates God's liberation of the Hebrew people from the oppression of their Egyptian overlords. In this awesome demonstration of power, God showed that God cared so much about the oppression the Hebrews were suffering that God personally came down to rip them out of the domination of the mightiest empire then known to humanity. God wanted to create a covenant community and made it clear that even the mightiest human empire was powerless to stop it from happening.

God was not content to tinker with the structures of the Egyptian Empire in order to make a place for the covenant people. Instead, God removed them from their oppression and brought them into a new land where they could realize God's dream for the ideal community. During their wanderings in the wilderness, the people learned that God was the ideal covenant partner who provided food and water and protected them from their enemies.

God and the people entered into a covenant relationship. The people learned God's personal name — Yahweh — and God's relentless demand for justice and right relationships. God's guidelines for this new community were given to the people through Moses. By accepting God's law as the guide for their community life, they began their journey with God.

Origins and ancestors

Genesis 1 – 2	The creation narratives: divine order
Genesis 3 – 5	The Fall: human disorder and its consequences
Genesis 6 – 11	Noah; the tower of Babel
Genesis 12 – 17	Abraham: called to create a covenant family
Genesis 18 – 23	Abraham; the city of Sodom
Genesis 24 – 35	Isaac, Esau, and Jacob
Genesis 37 – 50	Joseph

Why God would choose the Hebrews from among all the peoples of the earth is a perplexing mystery. The meaning of this divine election can be discovered only by placing it in some wider context. The book of Genesis provides two contexts to help us understand this covenant. The first is the context of God's relationship with all humanity; the second is the context of the Hebrew tribal traditions.

Genesis 1 – 11 puts the Hebrew story in the overarching context of God's choice of all humanity, in the person of Adam and Eve, to be God's covenant partner. The story sketches the recurring pattern of God's relationship with humanity: God initiates a relationship, which is then corrupted by human sin, thus evoking God's terrifying judgment and the loss of the divine gifts, followed by the crescendo of sinfulness that poisons all human relationships.

But God does not give up. Even when sin has so mangled creation that God decides to wipe it out, God spares Noah and his family, who embody the chosen community. Eventually, sin again reclaims the world as its own until humanity tries to demonstrate its equality with God by building a tower to ascend to God instead of waiting for God to come down to earth. God retaliates by confusing human language, thus frustrating the human ability to communicate with one another and create a unified community.

But God does not give up. Genesis 12 – 50 relates the divine invitation to Abraham and his family to create God's ideal covenant community. The thread of this hope, passing from Abraham to Isaac to Jacob in mysterious and surprising ways, reminded the Hebrews that God had been with them

A QUICK TOUR OF THE BIBLE

long before they knew who accompanied them on their journey. The story also relates how the Hebrew family ended up in Egypt because of Joseph and how God preserved them from harm. This also explains why the Hebrews were still in Egypt four hundred years later at the time of the exodus.

The Genesis narrative reveals that the stories of God's relation to humanity and to Israel follow essentially the same plot. Persons are called by God to become a community that is to be characterized by right relationships. But human sin breaks down the relationship and finally ruptures it, which leads to God's judgment. Since judgment is never the last word of a merciful and loving God, the relationship is restored only because God wants it to be. God is characterized by a relentless commitment to creation and an insatiable desire to relate with humanity.

Life with God in the Promised Land

Joshua 1 – 6; 23, 24	The conquest of the new land
Judges 4 – 8; 13 – 16	Charismatic leaders: Deborah, Gideon, and Samson
1 Samuel 1 – 15	Kingship: Samuel and Saul
1 Samuel 16 – 31; 2 Samuel 1	Saul and David
2 Samuel 2 – 12	David and Nathan
2 Samuel 13 – 20; 1 Kings 1 – 3	David and Absalom
1 Kings 8 – 12; 17 – 21; 2 Kings 1	Solomon; the divided kingdom; Elijah
2 Kings 2 – 13	Elisha and Athaliah
2 Kings 17 – 25	Fall of Samaria and Jerusalem; exile

God's presence not only creates the community but also unleashes the drama of its relationship with God. The historical books of the Old Testament report the exciting story of the Israelite community as it conquers the land (Joshua); structures itself in a loose confederation of twelve tribes under the guidance of charismatic judges (Judges); and then forms a magnificent kingdom under the leadership of David and Solomon (1 and 2 Samuel).

From this, the grandest time in the history of the Hebrew people, the story describes the breakup of the kingdom after Solomon's death into two kingdoms: Israel in the north (ten tribes) and Judah in the south (two tribes). Finally, the story culminates with the events leading to the annihilation of the northern kingdom by the Assyrians (721 B.C.) and the destruction of the southern kingdom by the Babylonians (587 B.C.), which resulted in the Hebrews' fifty-year exile (1 and 2 Kings).

In all of these political and social transformations, the guiding hand of God is evident. This is not just history, but salvation history — history that reveals God as present and active in the lives of people. God's providence and prophets ensure that, amidst the human schemes of power politics, God's design for the right way to live is never forgotten.

The New Testament Foundations: Jesus and Discipleship

Once you are familiar with the story of God's search for the right kind of community, you are ready to shift to the New

Testament. Reading the New Testament is much more meaningful when you are familiar with the broad outlines of this Old Testament story. The New Testament reveals God's new initiative — with Jesus — for the right kind of community and how the relationship is continued in Jesus' community of disciples. The twin questions that should always guide your reading of the New Testament are, Who is Jesus? and What does it mean to belong to his discipleship community?

The Gospels of Mark and Luke

Mark 1 – 3	Preparing the new way of relating to God
Mark 4:1 – 8:21	Building the new community for Jews and Gentiles
Mark 8:22 – 12:44	On the way to Jerusalem to suffer
Mark 14 – 16	The passion narrative
Luke 1 – 2 (Matthew 1 – 2)	The infancy narratives
Luke 3:1 – 9:50	Jesus' ministry in Galilee
Luke 9:51 – 19:27	Jesus' journey to Jerusalem
Luke 19:28 – 20:47; 22 – 24	Jesus' passion, death, and resurrection
Acts 1 – 12	The Church in its Jewish environment
Acts 13 – 28	The Church opens to the Gentiles

A good way to begin your New Testament reading is with the Gospel accounts of Jesus' life. Since Mark's Gospel was most probably the first one written, it is the first one to read. Mark's great achievement was to shape the many events of Jesus' life into a proclamation of the Christian message. He created a new form of literature that was more than a biography. It was a story of Jesus' life that proclaimed the gospel message. Mark gives Jesus' life a narrative shape and anchors Jesus' many sayings into particular situations in his story. Mark also stresses the importance of the ending, which is the good news that God, not death, triumphs. Mark's good news is that death ends Jesus' life but not his relationship with God. The resurrection shows that God's creative power to give life triumphs over evil's destructive desire to deal death.

Then read the two-volume work of Luke, which includes his Gospel and the Acts of the Apostles. Luke revises Mark's Gospel by adding many sayings and teachings that were either unknown or unavailable to Mark. He also adds infancy narratives to demonstrate how Jesus' mission and ministry are rooted in the Old Testament expectations of a messiah.

Most surprising of all, Luke adds a second volume to his Gospel, which we call the Acts of the Apostles, to show how the mission and ministry of Jesus is carried on by his community of disciples after his death. This exciting story traces the growth of the early Christian community from the Pentecost proclamation of Peter in Jerusalem to the missionary outreach of Paul to the Gentiles.

Paul and his letters

1 and 2 Thessalonians	Advice for converts to the Christian way
Philippians	Putting on the mind of Christ
1 Corinthians	The new Christian sacredness
2 Corinthians	The new Christian discipleship
Galatians	The new Christian freedom
Romans	The Gospel according to Paul
Colossians	Christ: Lord of the universe
Ephesians	The one Church: sign of the new creation
Philemon	Freedom in Christ

When you are familiar with the outline of Paul's career from the Acts of the Apostles, you can read his letters to the different Christian communities located in the cities of the Gentile world. Reading these letters gives you an inside view of life in these communities as the early Christians struggled to discover what it meant to be a Christian in a world that knew little and cared even less about Jesus.

Reading these letters in their chronological order also helps you appreciate the development of Paul's theological and practical understanding of Christian life. These letters also offer a window into Paul's personality. They lay bare how his personal experience of the risen Christ shaped his vision, sharpened his values, and guided his behavior.

John 1 – 4	Book of signs 1: Jesus and the response of faith
John 5 – 12	Book of signs 2: Jesus and the Jewish feasts
John 13 – 17	Book of glory 1: the farewell discourse
John 18 – 21	Book of glory 2: the passion, death, and resurrection

The Gospel of John demonstrates how different the Gospel accounts of Jesus' life can be. Although not directly based on Mark or any of the other Gospels, John's way of telling the good news of Jesus is rooted in the same Christian traditions. John's Gospel was composed near the end of the first century. It offers a unique perspective on the divinity of Jesus and on the nonhierarchical character of John's community. Jesus is the divine revealer who has come down from God to show us who God is and what God wants. He teaches in long speeches and performs distinctive signs that help us understand his message. Before he returns, he gives us the Holy Spirit to abide with us in his place.

Christian apocalyptic expectations

Another emphasis in early Christianity was what we describe as apocalyptic (from the Greek word meaning "to uncover or reveal"). Christian apocalypticism expresses the eager anticipation of God's total triumph over evil and the resulting foundation of a new order — a new creation — which would be free from oppression, injustice, violence, and suffering. This style of writing stresses that God's final transformation of our disordered world into a rightly ordered one is just around the corner.

Mark 13; Luke 21; Matthew 24 – 25	Apocalyptic discourses of Jesus before his death
Revelation 1 – 3	The vision of Christ in the Christian community
Revelation 4 – 11	The vision of Christ in the cosmos
Revelation 12 – 19:10	The vision of Christ in human history
Revelation 19:11 – 22:21	The vision of Christ and God's final victory

The book of Revelation is an imaginative description of what will happen when God comes to create justice in our unjust world. John describes his mystical journey into heaven. From this divine perspective, he is allowed to see how God's kingdom will come and how God's will will "be done, on earth as it is in heaven" (Matthew 6:10). Through his revelatory visions of Christ in the Christian community (chapters 1 – 3), of Christ in the cosmos (chapters 4 – 11), and of Christ in human history (chapters 12 – 22), John paints a vivid tableau of God's triumph through Christ and the final transformation of our world into the one that God envisioned from the beginning.

The Old Testament Revisited: Exile and Restoration

The next step in your reading journey is to return to the Old
Testament to learn more about the story of the Israelite community and its life in relationship to God. The Israelites' distinctive identity came from their covenant relationship with
God. But keeping the covenant was never an easy thing to do.
In fact, at one point their kingdom was destroyed, and they
were banished into exile. This devastating experience forced
them to rethink their relationship to God and to one another.
The exile (and the possible end of the covenant relationship)
and the relationship's unexpected restoration by God's power
are the focus of these readings.

The preexilic prophets

Amos	The prophet of social justice
Hosea	Covenant fidelity and infidelity
Isaiah of Jerusalem (Isaiah 1 – 39)	God's Word and power politics
Micah	Reformer from the country
Zephaniah	Hope beyond judgment
Nahum	God's justice for Assyria
Jeremiah	God's Word in crisis: judgment and hope

Reading the prophets will bring you back to the political and
social events that shaped and reshaped the Jewish community during the period from about 750 to 400 B.C. But these
crises are now perceived from the religious viewpoint of the

prophets rather than from the political viewpoint of the kings. As lobbyists for God's agenda for the right kind of community, the prophets warn kings and communities of the consequences of making decisions that are contrary to God's plan.

You will be challenged by Amos's demands for social justice and Hosea's daring portrait of God's faithfulness to the covenant despite the people's infidelity. Isaiah counsels kings to trust in God rather than in foreign alliances and demonstrates over and over that God's covenant demands have sobering consequences for those who disregard them. Sin brings God's judgment because God's holiness cannot be taken for granted. Micah, Zephaniah, and Nahum all develop angles on the double-edged proclamation of God's judgment of sin and our hope for restoration.

Jeremiah introduces us to the personal anguish of a spokesman for God. He proclaimed God's way of life to a community on its way to death. They were unwilling to listen and had no desire to hear and heed God's word. Jeremiah's powerful poetic images and personal prayers match the unimaginable and devastating reality of God's judgment on the kingdom of Judah.

Judah will be destroyed because it replaced the covenant obligations of fidelity and obedience with idolatry, infidelity, apostasy, and disobedience. The nation forgot its first-commandment obligation to center its life on God and instead organized life around objects that it thought it could control. Since the covenant has not been kept, God's destructive and punishing judgment is inevitable. Announcing this message makes Jeremiah sad because the people will not change and angry because his word is not listened to. He knows that without the people's conversion, there is no hope for a reversal of God's impending judgment.

But Jeremiah also sees clearly what nobody else can imagine: God does not give up. When all else fails, God will continue to be faithful, but in ways that demand death to the people's cherished institutions — the religious temple and the national kingdom. Jeremiah recognizes that God is now doing something that will entail a massive discontinuity with the whole past of the people. Their temple will be destroyed, their land will be taken away, and they will be displaced. But God will remain faithful to the covenant and establish a new covenant in the purified hearts of the people.

Jeremiah exemplifies the challenge of relating to God. His life illustrates the elusive, surprising, and mysterious ways in which God deals with each person. He shows how someone meets the challenges of each step in the process of relating to God: call, commitment, co-mission, conversion, and cost. His portrait is carefully constructed to help us to learn how faith is possible in a time of crisis. Jeremiah shows us through his words and actions what it means to be a prophet, one who hears the word of God and responds wholeheartedly. Despite the terrible cost to himself, Jeremiah was one willing do anything so that God would be recognized.

Exilic and postexilic prophets

Lamentations	The A to Z of suffering
Obadiah	Judgment for Judah's neighbors
Ezekiel	God's Word in the new situation of exile
Second Isaiah (Isaiah 40 – 55)	God's Word for a new creation
Haggai	Encouragement to rebuild the temple
Zechariah (1 – 8)	Oracles for rebuilding the temple
Third Isaiah (Isaiah 56 – 66)	Oracles for community restoration

In the depths of exile, the Jews faced the gravest crisis of their existence. What kind of a God had they tied themselves to? The exilic and postexilic prophets deal with this crisis of identity and meaning. During the exile, they asked the most haunting questions of all: Why did this happen to us? Was God absent or angry or maybe powerless to help?

Their answer produced a more sophisticated understanding of God as not merely one among many gods but as the only God there is. In response, the community focused on Torah, Territory, and Temple — being a holy people in a holy land with a holy dwelling place for God — to govern and guide every aspect of the community's restoration.

What do you do when your world is shattered? More important, what do you do when your dreams are shattered? Ezekiel is an example of a prophet who ministers in a situation of discontinuity. Discerning the meaning of new situations requires imaginative thinking. Ezekiel, whose personal weirdness is matched only by his zeal for God's ways, is the master of street theater. He proclaims God's message through his dramatic (and often erratic) behavior. Ezekiel first struggles to explain what God is doing by bringing about the exile and rejecting the covenant. Then — in memorable images such as a field of dry bones coming to life — he describes what God will do in the future to restore the covenant.

Ezekiel urges the people to understand that the process of their relation to God moves from calling to covenant, from commitment to obligation, from sin to judgment, and finally from punishment in exile to restoration. Though the covenant and its divinely given institutions — the temple and the monarchy — were lost through mismanagement, God would surprisingly restore the covenant community. This cycle now discloses the full pattern of God's plan for salvation. Knowing this, God's holy people can avoid the mistakes of the past that broke the covenant and provoked God's judgment.

Since it is impossible to realize what we cannot imagine, the Jewish exiles can't deal with freedom and a restored covenant without some preparation. So Second Isaiah, the author of chapters 40–66 of the book of Isaiah, marshals his poetic power to speak a word of comfort and to evoke in the imagination of his audience the astounding message of a new homecoming. From the depths of exile, Isaiah recognizes that God is doing something new.

In exile in Babylon, the Jews hear the rumors of world-shaking events. The dreaded Babylonian Empire is about to be crushed by the Persian armies of Cyrus the Great. In this crisis, God reminds the people that when God is with them, there is nothing to fear. Their future will be radically different because God is present in power to transform their exile into a homecoming — a new exodus experience.

Isaiah's exquisite poetry urges the people to participate in this new future with God. Isaiah recalls their history with God in order to reaffirm their identity. To renew their community, they must relive the exodus experience that formed them into a suitable covenant community for God. This poetry of God's new creation was one of the most frequently cited parts of the Old Testament for early Christians. No doubt they saw themselves as those who were living out the fulfillment of Isaiah's imaginative description of God's new creation.

On a more practical level, the prophets Haggai and Zechariah successfully focus the people's energy for the reconstruction of a new temple upon their return from exile. This second temple was begun about 536 B.C., amidst the poverty, chaos, and exploitation of the return from Babylon. The rebuilt structure was initially completed and dedicated in 515. It was constantly refurbished and updated until the time of Jesus. A lavish remodeling occurred during the time of King Herod the Great (37 – 4 B.C.). It was destroyed by the Romans in A.D. 70 and has never been rebuilt. Its original foundation stones make up the Wailing Wall on the temple mount in Jerusalem today.

The restoration after the exile

Ezra 1, 3 – 10	Restoring the holiness of the community
Nehemiah 1 – 2, 4 – 6, 8 – 10, 13	Rebuilding the people of God
1 Chronicles 10 – 22, 28 – 29	Restoration by retrieval of traditions
2 Chronicles 1 – 24, 28 – 36	A theologian's history
Joel	Natural disaster: from panic to prayer
Malachi	Teacher for the restored community
Ruth	Discovering the God of the ordinary

As always throughout human history, God's presence initiates a new relationship. So in the depths of despair and the silence of the Jewish exile, God spoke a new word of invitation, which invited the people into a new and restored relationship. This word empowered the exiles to shake off their oppression and be free. Delivered from its exile, the community could return to its land and restore its community life. It would be the community that God had always wanted. It would follow the guidelines of God's instructions (the Torah) and be centered on the presence of God in the people's midst (the temple). This reorganization required a rethinking of who God was and who they were as God's people.

Several biblical books chart the progress of the restoration and illustrate the holiness and careful observance of covenant obligations (Torah) that characterize the postexilic Jewish community. The books of Ezra and Nehemiah portray how the urgent desire to rebuild the walls of Jerusalem is coupled with the desire to build a spiritual wall of separation between the restored community and all other nations. Ezra tells the story from the priestly viewpoint, concentrating on the restoration of holiness to the temple, the land, and the people. Nehemiah tells it from the viewpoint of the Persian governor, struggling to rebuild the walls of Jerusalem and defend the land from its surrounding enemies.

God's covenant people demonstrated their concern for holiness by guarding the boundaries of their community, their nation, and their own bodies. These boundaries created a distinctive Jewish identity, which invited hostility from their neighbors and encouraged isolation and an inward-looking attitude. The book of Ruth, although set in the earlier time of King David, reflects some of the postexilic Jewish tension between being a closed and exclusive community or an open and inclusive one that would be more tolerant of outsiders and cooperative with its Gentile neighbors.

The books of 1 and 2 Chronicles are a revisionist history of the Jewish people seen through the lens of restoration. The author, or Chronicler, retells the history of the people from the books of Samuel and Kings, with particular restoration emphases. He stresses that religion dominates all other social institutions. What makes a great political leader is not his warfare, his wealth, his wisdom, or his concubines, but his essential faith commitment to God, his fidelity to Torah, and his worship in the Jerusalem temple. Everything else is secondary.

A second feature of this postexilic history is the author's attempt to show that the tiny minority of Judah and the exiles are the true inheritors of the promises to all Israel. Like any minority in any era, they conduct a massive campaign of persuasion to show that their minority viewpoint is really that of all true believers. But in order to appropriate for themselves what has previously belonged to all Israel, the Chronicler must account for why the line of descent can be traced to them alone. Just as in so many of the biblical stories where the younger brother or the unlikely one gets the inheritance, so the Chronicler indicates that the inheritance comes to them alone for their fidelity and their worship of God. The northern tribes have freely chosen to forsake their covenant relationship with God and so have become schismatics.

Amidst the difficulties of restoration, two prophetic teachers arise to help the people understand how to detect the Lord in their precarious struggles for identity and survival. Malachi reinforces the demand for holiness by teaching through short catechetical dialogues, while Joel uses oracles coupled with ritual to proclaim his message of God's special relationship and care for the people even in the midst of a devastating locust plague. The different approaches of these two prophets can help us discover how to make God's Word more applicable in our own situations.

Hebrew poetry and songs

Song of Songs	The dream of a loving relationship
Psalms	The five books of David's Torah
Psalms 1, 15, 22, 34, 51, 104, 119, 141	Hebrew poetry and its use in Christian liturgy
Psalms 3, 5, 6, 88	Individual laments
Psalms 14, 74, 80, 137	Communal laments
Psalms 32, 38, 130	Psalms of repentance
Psalms 109, 139:19 – 22	Curse psalms
Psalms 23, 27, 62, 91, 131	Psalms of confidence and trust
Psalms 30, 92, 116	Individual thanksgiving psalms
Psalms 65, 118, 124	Communal thanksgiving psalms
Psalms 8, 29, 33, 48, 100, 113, 148, 150	Psalms of praise
Psalms 2, 45, 72, 101, 110, 132	Royal psalms
Psalms 78, 105, 106, 135, 136	Reviewing the story of Israel through the psalms
Psalms 50, 82	Prophetic psalms
Psalms 37, 49	Wisdom psalms
Psalms 47, 95, 96	Psalms celebrating Yahweh as king
Psalm 89	A messianic psalm

Poets speak through the language of images. Images are the poet's way to make the invisible visible (which is always why we use images for God!). By using *metaphors* (from the Greek *metapherein,* "to carry over or transfer"), the poet helps us transfer the meanings of our familiar experience to a new and unfamiliar experience. The images of metaphorical language capture in concrete ways the many-layered complexity of an experience in order to evoke our own corresponding experiences (not just our ideas!). The poet's motto is "You had to be there — but since you weren't, I'll try to re-create the experience for you through my poem!"

The Song of Songs expresses the mystery and power of love and celebrates the whole range of experiences of being in love. The poet speaks through the language of images rather than with clinical or analytic detachment. By including this book in the canon of Scripture, we extend its meaning not only to the love of a man and a woman but also to God's love for us as a community and as individuals. Were this book not in our Bible, we might never imagine that God loves us so passionately!

The book of Psalms expresses the entire range of experiences and emotions the Jewish people encountered in their relationship with God. As the lyric expression of the prayer life of Israel, the psalms offer examples of the proper attitudes, values, and theology that the postexilic community celebrated in their lives and in their temple worship. The psalms are the poetic expression of the right way for the people to relate to God and to others.

As poems of our human spiritual experience, the psalms invite every human person and group to somehow share what they describe. Thus the psalms become examples to us (individuals or communities) of how we can respond to God, regardless of our situation. The psalms express the whole spectrum of our life experience: our orientation to God (hymns of praise and well-being in God's presence); our disorientation from God (songs of lament and loss); and our reorientation to God (hymns of thanks and restoration).

The psalms mirror our relationship with God and reflect the way that ancient people understood their relationships. The types of psalms reflect their understanding of the obligations of God and the community. Laments express when the relationship is not going well, either because God is perceived as distant and inactive or because we recognize that our sinfulness jeopardizes the relationship.

The hymns express when the relationship is going well because God has come near and acted with power to change our situation and save us. Hymns of praise declare our wonder and joy at God's mighty deeds, whether in history or in creation. The hymns' intent is to give honor to God, to shout God's praises and let everyone know what a wonderful God we have. Psalms of confidence or trust give form to our commitment to God and to our relationship with God. Psalms of thanksgiving signify our recognition of a gift bestowed by God, our heavenly benefactor.

Old and New Testaments Revisited: God's Word in the Hellenistic World

The final step on your reading journey follows the Jewish experience from the end of the exile until the time of Jesus, and the Christian experience of transition from a Jewish to a Gentile (non-Jewish) church. This stretch of history was divided into two periods, dominated first by the Persian Empire (538–333 B.C.) and then by the Greek, or Hellenistic, Empire resulting from the conquests of Alexander the Great (after 333).

During this time, the Jews struggled to maintain their distinctive religious identity despite being a colonial people under the domination of the superpowers of their day. In their homeland, they restored their temple and their social institutions under the guidance of their priests. Outside the Holy Land, in what the Jews called the diaspora (Greek for "dispersion"), scattered pockets of Jews established themselves especially in the larger cities that were springing up as the centers of Hellenistic cultural life. Greek culture and language became the universal standard for commerce and culture throughout the entire Mediterranean world. When Christianity emerged from Judaism in the first century A.D., it flourished especially in the cities where the diverse population was unified by its use of Greek.

The Old Testament books composed during this period reflect the culture war between Judaism and Hellenism.

Jewish texts reinforce Jewish identity and encourage Jews to be proud of their heritage. Traditional Jewish wisdom literature was transformed so that it could hold its own in dialogue with Hellenistic philosophy. Fictional heroes modeled genuine Jewish values and behavior. Many books promoted resistance, and some even outright revolt, against the toxic influence of Hellenistic culture.

The New Testament texts reflect the painful transition during the second half of the first century from Christian communities that were almost exclusively Jewish to ones that were mixed with non-Jews to ones that were almost exclusively Gentile. Coping with the problems of this transition, Christian authors like Matthew worked hard to retrieve their Jewish heritage to use it to meet the developing problems confronting them as they participated in the Christian mission spreading throughout the Hellenistic culture.

Wisdom in Israel

In the biblical library, the self-help section is called the wisdom literature. This collection helps people cope with the complexities of everyday life, especially sickness and suffering, death and disaster. It gives a practical understanding of how the world and society worked, and so helps a person understand who he or she is and how to fit into the larger scheme of things.

Since the wisdom literature did not rely on divine revelation but on practical experience and observation of nature, it formulated traditional advice for responsible living that the Jews shared with many ancient Near Eastern peoples. The Jews, though, sought to merge this secular tradition with the religious guidelines of their covenant instruction (Torah).

Proverbs 1 – 9	The worldview of wisdom
Proverbs 10, 16, 22 – 24, 28, 30 – 31	Wisdom in its cultural contexts
Habakkuk, Job 1 – 14	Questioning the accepted traditions
Job 15 – 28	Wisdom challenged: God on trial
Job 29 – 42	God on trial: The Creator's defense
Ecclesiastes (Qoheleth)	The failure of wisdom
Sirach (Ecclesiasticus) 1 – 4, 14 – 18, 20 – 23	Wisdom reaffirmed
Sirach 24 – 26, 30, 34 – 36, 38 – 39, 42 – 51	Torah and wisdom are one
Wisdom	Praise of wisdom and God's constant fidelity

The book of Proverbs consists of short, memorable sayings, shaped poetically for memory and meaning and drawn from human experience. Since they are practical, proverbs serve many functions for people in their communities, including observation, command, admonition, and prohibition. In general, they help to preserve tradition, ponder the mysteries of life, and promote proper behavior.

Not only are the images and messages memorable, but the shape of the proverbs is poetic. In particular, Hebrew wisdom utilizes the parallelism of couplets to juxtapose truths and tease out new meanings. Good proverbs are characterized by being memorable, true to experience, practical or useful, and universally applicable.

Each proverb is like a snapshot of a vast panorama that needs to be complemented by other viewpoints. Since no proverb can totally capture the complexity of life's mystery, the truth of each must be taken in context with that of others to create the whole picture. For the ancients, "proof" for a claim or position often came from quoting the best or most appropriate proverb. (For an example of this, see the story of Jesus and the Syrophoenician woman in Mark 7:24 – 30.)

The patron of wisdom is Solomon, whose Hebrew name is related to peace, "shalom." Peace is the result of living in harmony with the comprehensive order that God created and that is the ideal for the community that lives according to God's will.

The prophet Habakkuk, the just sufferer Job, and the skeptical Ecclesiastes, or Qoheleth, represent the probing, questioning, dark side to this wisdom material. Qoheleth and Job relentlessly question the working of God's justice. Both share the perspective that life is twisted; their experience verifies that too often good people suffer and the wicked prosper. They conclude that God must be responsible for the twisting!

So a real question about God emerges. Job is optimistic and believes that we can know how and why God acts. Qoheleth is pessimistic and thinks that we cannot know

A way to summarize some of the basic wisdom themes is to re-member that Wisdom builds her house on seven pillars (Proverbs 9:1), which is also the number of letters in Solomon's English name!

S uccessful living comes through acquiring wisdom.

O rder was implanted in the cosmos at creation by God and discovered through wisdom.

L ife to the fullest — physical, social, economic, and spiritual — is the result of wisdom.

O ur world is a struggle against the forces of chaos, and this brings suffering and death.

M eaning can be challenged by our experience, but trust in God can overcome doubt.

O nly one God means that creation and history can be united in one system.

N o one who finds wisdom will be cut off from deathless fellowship with God.

these things. In the book of Job there is a shift from the tra-ditional view that God is just and must reward good and punish evil in this life to a view that God's ways are right and just but we will never know exactly how.

The book of Ecclesiastes, or Qoheleth, finds that life is without justice and concludes that it is hollow and that death is preferable. Since death is the final end of everything and there are no guarantees of how anything will work out after one has died, trying to control things or change things is futile. Why bother to look to the future, which no one can control? Instead, concentrate on getting whatever little pleasures have fallen to you.

The books of Sirach and Wisdom reinstate the traditional wisdom by incorporating it into the Jewish religious worldview. The instructions of secular wisdom and of religious law can be united because there is only one God, who is both the creator of the universe and the lord of salvation history. These later wisdom books encourage Jews to seek for wisdom not only in creation but also in the history of their relationship to God.

Sirach rethinks his wisdom theology in the light of God's revealed will found in the Law. Since there is only one God, there can be only one divine guideline for the people, whether it is expressed in the order of creation or the explicit commands of Torah. Wisdom's task is to appreciate God's providence and power both as creator and as lord of history.

The book of Wisdom combines the Jewish traditions of creation and salvation history with Hellenistic forms of thought. It speaks to a broad spectrum of Jews. To faithful Jews, it offers an integration of creation and God's law. To wavering Jews, it encourages fidelity to their ancestral traditions that set them apart from other peoples. To unfaithful Jews, it invites a return to their religious traditions. To non-Jews, it offers a persuasive argument about the integrity and superiority of Jewish religious wisdom.

Jonah	Prophet of divine mercy
Esther	Courage for Jews in the diaspora
Tobit	Jewish identity in the diaspora
Baruch	Jewish spirituality in the diaspora
Zechariah 9 – 14	Messianic expectations
1 Maccabees 1 – 9	Narrative of the revolt (167 – 64 B.C.)
2 Maccabees 1 – 7, 9 – 10, 12:38 – 46; 15	Interpreting the revolt for Egyptian Jews
Judith	An example of resistance during persecution
Daniel 1 – 6, 13 – 14	Tales of fidelity to God in the diaspora
Daniel 7 – 12	Apocalyptic hopes for changing the world

As Hellenism spread throughout the Mediterranean world
after the conquests of Alexander the Great, who died in 323
B.C., Jewish identity was threatened both in the diaspora
(as Jews called the world outside the Holy Land) and in their
homeland. The threat was not so much to eliminate their
Jewishness but to change it so radically that it no longer existed
as genuine Jewishness. Diaspora Jews, who lived outside the
Holy Land amidst Gentiles, were confronted with serious
challenges to their Jewish lifestyle. Their primary question
was whether a Jew could be Hellenistic and still remain a Jew.

The core of Jewish identity was their election to be God's covenant people. This covenant relationship and its obligations set them apart from other peoples. So the Jews defined a countercultural lifestyle that opposed Hellenism through literature of cultural resistance and politics of national resistance.

Several biblical books reflect this conflict between the Jewish lifestyle and the Hellenistic culture in which they lived. Jonah, Esther, Tobit, and Baruch offer readers concrete examples of the lofty ideals of Jewish spirituality that could flourish in a pagan environment. These books offer examples that served as guidelines for being a Jew in the Greek world.

The books of 1 and 2 Maccabees tell the story of political defiance during the years 168 – 164 B.C., when Jewish resistance exploded into a successful revolution against the Greek ruler Antiochus IV Epiphanes. The Maccabees provide an example of armed resistance — the Jews' "holy war" to defend their land and make sure it remained holy.

The books of Daniel and Judith also come from this revolutionary period. Daniel combines examples of God's care for faithful Jews in their hostile environment and depictions of the eventual triumph of God over evil in our world. This book offers hope in times of crisis because it shows that God will always intervene to deliver the chosen people who remain faithful to the covenant. The book of Judith uses a fictional story to encourage resistance and promote the desire for Jewish freedom.

Christianity in the Hellenistic world

Matthew 1 – 4	Matthew's Gospel: guide for Christian discipleship
Matthew 5 – 7	Jesus' Sermon on the Mount
Matthew 8 – 10	The gospel of the kingdom comes in power
Matthew 11 – 17	Alternative responses to the kingdom of heaven
Matthew 18 – 23	The new relationship under stress
Matthew 24 – 28	The turning of the ages
1 and 2 Timothy, Titus	Handing on the Pauline legacy
James	Teaching Christian wisdom
Jude	Defending faith and tradition
1, 2, and 3 John	Coping with dissension and division
1 and 2 Peter	Belonging, and encouragement for a new life
Hebrews	Jesus: mediator of all and eternal High Priest

The early Christians also had problems living in the Hellenistic culture. The Gospel of Matthew, the letter to the Hebrews, and the pastoral and Catholic letters show how various communities dealt with problems concerning authority, leadership, doctrine, moral behavior, and organization in the newly formed communities. These books also illustrate the development of Christianity in the first century from a loosely organized group to a more structured community.

Matthew revised Mark's gospel life of Jesus for a Jewish community that was confronted by the influx of Gentiles who were taking over the Church after Paul's missionary success. He shaped his Gospel to teach his community to embrace its Jewish tradition because this tradition was the foundation of the Christian way of life. But he also stressed that the community's future task was participation in the Church's evangelizing mission to the Gentiles. By portraying Jesus as both the fulfillment of the hopes of Judaism and as the inaugurator of the new Christian way of relating to God, Matthew's Gospel serves as a powerful tool for conversion and co-mission for his Christian community.

The pastoral letters are the later Pauline letters. They portray Paul as an aging pastor whose final care for the community is expressed by appointing successors to continue his work. They claim Paul's authority for the growing institutionalization of the Church. These letters have always been grouped together (they might even have been written as a group) and are best read in the order of 1 Timothy, Titus, and 2 Timothy. They relate Paul's advice for establishing similar administrative offices and pastoral traditions both for communities that he had founded (Timothy in Ephesus) and for communities that he did not found (Titus on Crete).

The letter to the Hebrews and the catholic letters of Peter, James, John, and Jude sketch how different communities confronted the problems of defining a Christian way of life in a world that was often hostile to their beliefs and behaviors. Since the Christian Church today still struggles to discover authentic applications of the gospel message for our times, these letters offer models for our search for suitable answers to today's complex problems.

Where Do You Go from Here?

Once you have finished your general tour through the Bible, the real adventure begins. Just as the journey to a new country cannot be limited to following the normal tourist agenda, so our biblical journey cannot be limited to a onetime reading. We must go back again and again to learn all we can about the people, places, and events of the biblical world.

Your local public or academic library contains many books on the Bible written by competent, scholarly guides. One way to begin your more detailed study is to choose a biblical book that you would like to know more about. Then choose a beginning or intermediate commentary and begin to work your way through it. Discover the authors who speak not only to your mind but also to your heart.

Although it is important to see the major tourist attractions, getting off the beaten path allows you to discover and appreciate much more fully the experience of those who live there. So after your initial reading, stop being a tourist. Get off the bus and go where you want! Don't be afraid to wander from the well-trodden paths to search out and explore something that really interests you. Ask the questions that fascinate you. Follow your own pathways and discover the surprises that God has waiting for you through your Bible reading.

Questions for Reflection and Group Discussion

1. *What are the benefits of beginning your Bible reading with the Exodus experience rather than the book of Genesis?*
2. *What is the significance of each of the two major parts of the book of Genesis (chapters 1–11 and 12–50)?*
3. *Describe the role of the Old Testament prophets. How would this description be an apt way to describe the work of Jesus?*
4. *Explain to a friend what a gospel is.*
5. *What was the purpose of the wisdom literature? Would it still be helpful today? Why or why not?*

MAKING YOUR JOURNEY

CHAPTER TEN

How to Read the Bible

Anytime we pick up the Bible, we can usually read the words. Our problems and disagreements are not about what the words say but rather about what they mean. Reading for meaning is a skill that, like any other, must be learned and developed through practice.

Learning to read for the meaning of Scripture must always be our goal. We desire not merely to recognize the words but to understand their meaning so that we can apply it to our life. Reading any text, especially an ancient one like the Bible, can be challenging. So it might be helpful to think about the reading process so that we can get the most out of it.

Reading for Meaning

Normally we read so habitually that it seems as if the words of the text leap from the page into our minds with immediate clarity. Because we have clear ideas, we assume that those ideas must be the ones the author intended by the words on the page. So we might think that reading the Bible will be as easy as reading our daily newspaper. We forget that reading our newspaper is a skill that has been mastered over many years of practice. To do it well we need some specialized skills to deal with the different types of writing we encounter.

"Read often, and study as much as you can;
let sleep overtake you with a book in your hand;
when your head nods, may it sink on a holy page."

— *ST. JEROME*
Letter 22

We hardly ever notice the many subtle shifts that we automatically make as readers when we're reading the newspaper. Each kind of writing (which in literary terms is called its form, or *genre*) guides the way we read it. As we move from the front page to sports, business and stock reports, comics, editorials, entertainment, and so forth, each type of writing triggers different expectations and demands special strategies for deciphering it.

Reading the Bible requires this same kind of skill. The content or message of the Bible always comes packaged in some specific literary form. Since the Bible is not just one book but a collection of many books featuring various types of writing (poetry, narratives, proverbs, letters, and so forth), each book creates expectations that require a specific reading strategy to determine that book's distinctive meanings. Furthermore, the different types of writing function to entertain, inform, persuade, and move us to action. So when we read the Bible, we must attend not only to the content (what is said) but also to the form (how it is said) and the function (why it is said) of each book.

Reading is an essential way of forming and reforming ourselves. Bible reading contributes to this because it demands a new type of involvement. As seekers, we cannot just skim the surface, amassing bits of unconnected information. Despite promises we often hear, there is no instant wisdom. Genuine wisdom requires the patient process of seeing the connections between facts and relating them to form the bigger picture. Biblical literacy is measured by assimilation, not accumulation.

Reading for meaning demands that we discover how what we read connects with what we experience. Reading a sacred book that we believe reveals the person and activity of God requires penetrating beyond the surface to the hidden depths of reality. Since the Bible mediates between our familiar world and that of a richer spiritual world infused with God's presence, by learning to read the Bible we learn to read our lives at a deeper, spiritual level.

The ABCs of Bible Reading

Our goal in reading the Bible is to let it change us so that we can live our relationships with God and with others in a fuller, Christian way. It helps to have a handy method as we go about our task of reading. Over my many years of teaching Scripture to adults, I have developed a procedure for reading Scripture that makes it as easy as ABC! This technique focuses on the three basic steps of our reading:

- Approaching the text
- Breaking open the text
- Connecting the text to our life

If we follow these steps, we will pay attention to all the factors necessary to arrive at an adequate interpretation of any text.

In order to understand this ABC method, let's take a specific biblical text to work with. Find the book of the Acts of the Apostles in your New Testament. Turn to chapter 8, verses 26 – 40 for the story of Philip the deacon and the Ethiopian pilgrim who is reading the book of Isaiah on his way home from Jerusalem. I've chosen this story of a reader and a seeker because it is a lot like our own. It also illustrates the ABC method in action.

Approaching the text: Examining our assumptions

What we get out of a text depends largely on what we bring to it as a reader. We always start with our own assumptions and our own reading skills. Our personal attitudes, experiences, knowledge, intelligence, desires, needs, and abilities influence our reading. The written words are fixed on the page and are the same for everybody. But different readers discover different meanings.

> "For as the divine Word stimulates the wise with mysteries, so it often kindles the simple with an obvious statement."
>
> — *POPE GREGORY I (THE GREAT)*
> Letter to Leander (ca. A.D. 594)

If you have ever discussed Scripture with a group or debated with someone trying to convert you, you know how true this is. Everybody reads the same verses, but they discover very different meanings. Some of this dissimilarity arises from the personal differences in knowledge and experience that readers bring to their interpretation of the text. Other differences arise from the interests that guide their reading and from the connections they make between the text and their lives.

When we read the Bible, we approach the text with two levels of assumptions. First, we bring a whole set of background assumptions about ourselves as readers, about the text as sacred, and about the process of interpretation. But we also are guided by more immediate assumptions about finding some meaning in this text for our lives.

Becoming aware of these background assumptions is the general preparation, remote from the immediate reason we might pick up this text. But these general assumptions guide everything we do, even if we do not consciously attend to them. This remote (as opposed to immediate) preparation is something we might have done years ago, yet it still influences our reading now. The reflections we have been doing in this book were designed to help us clarify our thinking about these assumptions. Although they are seldom spelled out in complete detail, these background assumptions influence every step of our reading journey. Unless we become more conscious of them at some point, they are liable to distort our reading. How would assumptions distort our reading? For one thing, assumptions often cover up the limitations of our own viewpoint. For another, assumptions arise from our own prejudices and will, through interpretation, tend to strengthen rather than correct our prejudices.

Whenever we want to read the Bible, we can get to the root of our more immediate personal assumptions by asking some basic questions about what we are seeking from our Bible reading. Notice that these questions are "now" directed and do not even recognize how many other assumptions about reading and about the Bible are influencing us even now!

- What is going on in my life that points me toward the Bible?
- Why would I want to read it and not some other book?
- What do I want or expect to discover from this reading?

MAKING YOUR JOURNEY

- What questions, concerns, or needs do I wish to answer or to clarify?

When we become conscious of our personal reasons for reading the Bible, we become more aware of our focus as we read the text. We can focus on the theological issue of who God is or how God acts, or on historical issues about when and where the events described happened, or on psychological issues — about what motivations or values prompted the people's choices. We can also focus on the application for our own problems by seeing how the biblical story is our story. In short, there is no end to the approaches we can take to a text.

"Owing to the depth of Scripture itself, everyone does not receive it in one and the same sense, but one in one way and another in another interprets the declarations of the same writer, so that it seems possible to elicit from it as many opinions as there are people."

—*VINCENT OF LERINS*
Commonitorium, II.5 (A.D. 434)

Breaking open the text: What it says and means

Good reading demands both an understanding of the words used and some context for identifying their meaning. Breaking open the meaning of a text demands two stages. Our first task in reading any text is to pay close attention to what it says. The best way to do this is to read the selected biblical passage all the way through without looking at any footnotes or other material. Sit quietly with the reading for a minute, reflecting on it. If there are words or phrases or religious terms that are not clear, look them up in a dictionary or a Bible dictionary. Note also what type of writing it is. At the least, determine whether it is prose or poetry.

After we know what the text says, we are ready to answer the question of what the text means. Since the text is a communication from an author to an audience, our first question is always, What did this passage mean to its author and the first readers? Determining what the author originally meant for a biblical passage is not always easy because it was composed centuries ago in a culture and language that was very different from ours. But we can always find help from scholars who know a lot more about history and the Bible than we do.

"Catholic exegesis does not claim any particular scientific method as its own. It recognizes that one of the aspects of biblical texts is that they are the work of human authors, who employed both their own capacities for expression and the means which their age and social context put at their disposal. Consequently, Catholic exegesis freely makes use of the scientific methods and approaches which allow a better grasp of the meaning of texts in their linguistic, literary, socio-cultural, religious and historical contexts, while explaining them as well through studying their sources and attending to the personality of each author."

—*PONTIFICAL BIBLICAL COMMISSION*
The Interpretation of the Bible in the Church (1993)

We notice these two stages as we read the story of the Ethiopian. The Ethiopian can easily grasp what the words of the scroll say, but their meaning eludes him. Without some indication of what the words are referring to, the passage is confusing and remains a puzzle. At this moment, through the direction of the Holy Spirit, the deacon Philip comes along-side the chariot. He asks whether the man understands what he is reading. The Ethiopian responds in words that express our need too: "How can I, unless someone instructs me?" (Acts 8:31, NAB).

The Ethiopian assumes that there is some meaning here, but he cannot determine what it is because he does not know to whom the words refer. He lacks the proper context that is required to furnish the meaning. But notice that he also realizes that discovering that meaning demands asking first what the author was trying to communicate — "I beg you, about whom is the prophet saying this?" (Acts 8:34, NAB). The Ethiopian knows that reading for meaning always hinges on knowing what the author was trying to say to the original audience.

Supplying this context of the original author is not some-thing we can always do easily on our own. So the Ethiopian welcomes the help of Philip's more specialized knowledge to supply this meaning. The meaning emerges when Philip puts this particular passage into the wider context of salvation history. The text becomes a springboard for Philip's proclamation of Jesus as the fulfillment of this "suffering servant" described by Isaiah (Isaiah 52:13–53:12).

Like the Ethiopian, we often need help from scripture scholars to discover what the text meant for the original author and audience. The footnotes in our Bible usually give us this help, and commentaries aid us when we have further questions. Once we have a sense of what the text meant to its author and its first readers, we can connect that meaning to similar situations and needs in our own life. In the next chapter, we will explore some ways that scholars can help us with problems that arise in our reading.

Connecting with the text: Applying it to life

Reading changes us. When we make the text our own, we are changed by what we discover. Books have different effects on us. Sometimes we read a novel and enjoy the story and then never think of it again. But some books and their meanings become important to us. We make them our own when we let their ideas shape our ideas, their values become ours, and their imperatives guide our actions.

"Conversion is the change of our lives that comes about through the power of the Holy Spirit. All who accept the Gospel undergo change as we continually put on the mind of Christ by rejecting sin and becoming more faithful disciples in his church. Unless we undergo conversion, we have not truly accepted the Gospel."

— *U.S. BISHOPS*
"Go and Make Disciples" (1992)

The connection between the biblical text and our life can take a variety of forms. Since the guiding assumptions and the interests chosen for reading it can be so varied, so will the applications. If, for example, we are expecting the Bible to supply us with a blueprint for our day, then our connections will need to be complex and highly artificial. If we want the Bible to provide some insight into what it means to be a Christian in an apparently uncaring or increasingly hostile world, then our connecting points will be more numerous and easier to discover.

Since we can connect with the text at any point and in any way, we need to narrow our focus in order to gain a specific benefit from our reading. One way to do this is to focus on either the people or the story.

If we focus on the people, then we look for how their ideas, feelings, values, and behavior might relate to our own. Every person we encounter in the Bible is like us. The root of the similarity is that both they and we are involved in a relationship with God. Their examples of how they worked out the details of living that relationship provide some clues for how we can do it too.

So when we read about the Ethiopian, we can connect his example as a seeker with our own search. We are encouraged to seek and find as he did, to read with perseverance when difficulties arise, to look for help when needed, to share our learning with others, and to respond generously when we discover God who speaks through the words of the text.

If we focus on the story, then we seek connecting points between the biblical story and our life story. The Bible is the story of people in relationship to God. The relationship moves through patterns: invitation and call; hearing and response; faith commitment and covenant; community and shared responsibility to build the relationship; challenges of meeting obligations and changing ourselves because of the relationship; and accepting the cost that maintaining the relationship demands. Where are we in this dynamic process of relationship with God? What are the challenges and demands that the biblical text opens to us? How does the text help us live more fully our relationship with God?

In the story of the Ethiopian, we discover the path that he follows into a deeper relationship with God through his Scripture reading. The journey begins with his desire to read the Bible. It continues with his searching out not only what the words say but also what they meant to their original author. It includes his willingness to rely on help from others and to share his search with them, and it finally culminates with his fearlessly changing his life because of what he read. His journey is our journey too.

As we read the Bible more often and in different circumstances, we discover that there is never just one meaning for any text. Likewise there is never just one application to our lives. As the situations in which we read the Bible change, so will our applications. Though the words of the text remain the same, their significance for today changes with our needs and interests as readers and with the circumstances in which we read them. This is why the Bible will continue to be read and interpreted anew throughout the lifetime of the Church.

"It's not what I don't understand in the Bible that bothers me—but what I do understand."

—MARK TWAIN

As We Work on God's Word, It Works on Us

As we use the ABC method to read the Bible for its meanings, we will notice that interpreting God's Word is not a one-sided process. God's Word is "living and active, sharper than any two-edged sword, piercing until it divides soul from spirit, joints from marrow; it is able to judge the thoughts and intentions of the heart" (Hebrews 4:12). Since God's Word is part of the communication of a relationship, it involves a give-and-take through which we are changed. Reading the Bible is like a conversation of transformation.

When we approach the Bible text, God is approaching us through that text. As we break open the meaning of the text, God breaks us open through the Word so that we can be transformed. And as we connect the text to our life, God connects us more closely to God through the words that we read. As we work on God's Word, God's Word works on us.

For our reading journey through the Bible, besides understanding the information or message of the biblical books, we need to use this information to live a better Christian life. As with the Ethiopian, merely gaining an intellectual insight is never the end of the process of Bible reading. When he discovers the meaning of the passage of Isaiah and its relation to Christ, he moves from information to action. He wishes to be baptized as a response to his reading. So our reading of Scripture is never simply for information but for the formation of ourselves as Christians. Reading is for living, and reading the Bible is for living in relationship with God.

Questions for Reflection and Group Discussion

1. *Share an example from your life of someone's meaning changing when his or her words were taken out of their original context.*
2. *Why is the identification of the type of writing, or genre, of a text so important in reading?*
3. *In your approach to the Bible, what questions, concerns, or needs prompt your search?*
4. *Why is the question of the meaning for the author and first readers of a text so important?*
5. *How come there can be so many different applications of a Bible text?*

CHAPTER ELEVEN

How Scripture Scholars Can Help Readers

Using the ABC approach for reading and interpreting equips us to become more competent readers of the biblical texts. However, it does not eliminate all the problems that we face as readers. Since reading is communication between an author and an audience, we must be sensitive to the problems that can arise in this communication process.

Contexts of Meaning: The Three Worlds of the Text

The three elements of author, audience, and text remind us that successful communication always joins three distinct worlds of meaning: the world of the author behind the text; the world within the text itself; and the world of the reader who is facing the text. When these worlds or their relationships change, so do the meanings of the text.

THE THREE WORLDS OF THE TEXT

1. *The world behind the text.* This is the world of the author and the original audience. This is the historical situation in which the author composed the text as a response to some particular problem or need of the audience.

2. *The world within the text.* This is the world described and portrayed within the text itself. This world can be self-contained, but normally we connect this world with our own world in order to apply its meaning to our own situation.

3. *The world facing the text.* This is the present situation of the person who is reading the text. Since a text endures through time once it is written down, this world changes with each historical situation of later readers.

The world behind the text

This is the historical and cultural world in which the author and the original readers lived and in which the text originated. Exploring this world helps us understand the situation of the author and the original readers, in particular the problems and issues that motivated the author to write the text. Every text is some kind of response or answer in a particular situation. Authors seldom write for posterity, but rather for someone now who will read their work and appreciate its meaning. No one writes to be misunderstood!

We explore this world using historical methods to answer questions about what was going on at the time of the writing (for example, the identity of the author and audience, the date and location of composition, the historical situation, the reasons for the text's composition, and so forth). Since the answers to these questions depend on the methods and procedures of historical scholarship, they are always open to further revision whenever the results of scholarship are updated and the methods of inquiry are improved.

For the Old Testament, this world behind the text is that of the Hebrew people during the twelve hundred years before Christ. Such a long period of history reveals many different social, political, and religious situations in which the various biblical books were written. Knowing the general framework of this historical development is helpful for situating the various books in their proper historical contexts.

For the New Testament, the texts are situated in the first-century Mediterranean world. The books and letters describe various situations in the Hellenistic Roman world, especially in the areas of Palestine, Syria, Asia Minor (present-day Turkey), Greece, and Rome. Some authors give important clues about their location and their audience, as does Paul in his letter introductions and John in the opening chapter of the book of Revelation. For others, scholars must sift through their texts to tease out clues about their original historical situations.

For general background on the historical, political, and social situations of the Old Testament, consider H. Jagersma, *History of Israel* (volume 1: Beginnings to 330 B.C.; volume 2: 330 B.C. to A.D. 135, Fortress Press). For the New Testament,

HOW SCRIPTURE SCHOLARS CAN HELP READERS

see John J. Rousseau and Rami Arav, *Jesus and His World: An Archaeological and Cultural Dictionary* (Fortress Press).

The world within the text

Texts create worlds of meaning. When we read them, they invite us to enter into those worlds. Biblical texts also create worlds of meaning, and when we step inside we are confronted by people, settings, and theological claims that are often strange and always challenging. Readers discover these textual worlds by a careful and critical reading of the text itself — regardless (at least at first!) of any information about the author or the original situation in which the text was composed. We are familiar with textual worlds from reading novels, in particular historical sagas or science fiction in which the story world describes a situation that is different from ours or the author's.

The textual world of the Old Testament book of Exodus, for example, is set in Egypt, very likely in the thirteenth century before Christ. The story describes the conflict between God's agent Moses and the Pharaoh, which leads to the liberation of the oppressed Hebrews from their bondage. Although the story as we have it in our Bible was written down long after the events, the story world retains its integrity because everything in it fits together.

The textual world of the Gospels is that of Jesus' lifetime during the first third of the first century. The story takes place mostly in the Jewish homeland in Galilee and its surrounding areas in Judea and Jerusalem around the years A.D. 27 – 30. This world is not the same as that of the four evangelists who wrote forty to sixty years later in greatly different circumstances. Yet the world of Jesus is consistent and coherent for any reader approaching the text.

Investigating the world within the text utilizes all our familiar skills of reading. Although literary scholars have developed very sophisticated techniques for appreciating the intricacies of textual communication, a simple method for exploring a text is to ask some basic questions:

- What kind of writing is this (form)?
- How does the writing fit together (structure)?
- Who is doing what, where, when, and why (story)?

These questions lead to an initial appreciation of the message (content) that the text communicates.

For more on the literary approach to the Bible, see Robert Alter and Frank Kermode, eds., *The Literary Guide to the Bible* (Harvard University Press) or David E. Aune, *The New Testament in Its Literary Environment* (Westminster / John Knox Press).

The world facing the text

This is the world of the reader or audience. Because a text becomes permanent through writing, it is available to other audiences besides the immediate community for whom it was composed. The world of the reader shifts constantly

SOME EXAMPLES OF TEXTS AND THEIR THREE WORLDS

Text	World within Text (STORY)	World behind Text (AUTHOR)	World facing Text (AUDIENCE OR READERS)
Pasternak's *Dr. Zhivago*	Russia, 1917	Italy, 1957	original audience anytime in history United States, 1990s
Dickens' *Tale of Two Cities*	French Revolution, 1790s	England, 1859	same
Shakespeare's *Julius Caesar*	Rome, 44 B.C.	London, ca. 1600	same
Mark's Gospel	Galilee, ca. A.D. 30	Rome, ca. A.D. 70	same
Paul's letters to the Corinthians	Corinth, A.D. 50s	Corinth, A.D. 50s	same
John's book of Revelation	Asia Minor, ca. A.D. 95 and a timeless mystical journey	Patmos and Ephesus (Roman province of Asia), ca. A.D. 95	same

as the text is read in many different historical times and social circumstances.

When we read the Bible now, almost nineteen hundred years after its last books were written, like the original audience, we are reading for clues about who God is and for cues about how to respond to our own experience of God's transforming presence. But the world in front of the text is now our own everyday reality, along with the various modern presuppositions and expectations we bring to our reading.

Reading for meaning connects the three worlds of the author, the audience, and the text. A satisfactory interpretation of any text demands some attention to each of these three worlds and to the relationships between them. Neglecting one of these worlds or failing to bridge the gaps that arise between them skews our interpretation and assures that our understanding will be incomplete.

Problems of Disconnected Worlds

In general, interpretation becomes difficult for Bible readers because gaps develop that separate one or another of the three worlds that were originally so closely connected at the time of composition. Scholars are ever hard at work devising ways to overcome these gaps.

The language gap

The language gap occurs because of the difference between the original language of the author and that of readers today. Since few of us read Hebrew, Greek, or Aramaic, we rely on the increased understanding of ancient languages and more sophisticated methods of translation employed by textual scholars and linguists who provide us with careful and critical modern translations of the biblical texts. This gap is primarily overcome by using one of the excellent modern translations that we discussed in chapter 8.

If you are interested in learning more about what textual scholars and translators do, see J. Harold Greenlee, *Introduction to New Testament Textual Criticism* (Rev. ed., Hendrickson) or Philip Wesley Comfort, *The Complete Guide to Bible Versions* (Tyndale House).

The historical gap

Once a text is written down, it takes on a life of its own. Later readers can read it in historical situations that are different from that of the first readers. Throughout history, Christians have continued to read the Bible because they believed that these sacred texts continued to be trustworthy and relevant guides for leading a Christian life. The Bible's importance is not limited to the first Christians as they worked out their faith and relationships. It is still applicable to our lives today.

The historical gap between the past and the present arises from this difference between the original situation and that of the present reader. When the text was first written, the author and readers shared the same situation. The world behind the text and the world facing the text were so close that connecting them was not too complicated. Knowing what the author meant was easier because they already shared so much about their everyday world. But when the world of the author and the world of the audience become disconnected, readers need more sophisticated strategies to figure out what the author meant when the text was composed.

Most critical biblical scholarship for the last century and a half has been guided by this quest to discover the original meaning of the text — what it meant to the author and the original audience for which it was intended. But since the world of the original biblical author and audience was so different from our own, biblical scholars have had to devise a general method of interpreting texts that recognizes this historical and cultural difference and tries to overcome it.

This method of reading is called the historical-critical method. The historical-critical method is *historical* because it attempts to understand the meaning of ancient texts in their original context (in relation to the historical, social, and literary situations in which they originated). It is *critical* because it compares and analyzes in order to arrive at historical and literary judgments about the results of the study.

The historical-critical method is primarily concerned with reading texts, especially ancient ones. It is based on the principle that any adequate reading requires attention to historical issues — who (author) addresses whom (audience) in what circumstances (situation) — and issues of literary criticism — in what way (form) with what message (content) for what reason (function). These basic questions structure the historical-critical method and contribute to its primary goal of learning what the text meant to its author and first readers.

If you are interested in understanding more about the historical-critical method of biblical scholarship, you might wish to read Raymond E. Brown, *The Critical Meaning of the Bible* (Paulist); Richard N. Soulen, *Handbook of Biblical Criticism: Revised and Expanded* (Westminster/John Knox Press); or Gordon D. Fee, *New Testament Exegesis* (Westminster/John Knox).

The cultural gap

Reading ancient texts, in particular those like the Bible that are also sacred, challenges us in many ways. The differences between the ancient world of the author and the original readers and our own world are not immediately apparent to us. The social and cultural world of those ancient people is like a strange country, where life is organized differently. Unless we gain some knowledge about their world, we can never hope to understand what they understood and were trying to communicate.

Our world is vastly different from the New Testament world of two thousand years ago and even further removed from the Old Testament world of Judaism. The danger for readers today is that we tend to confuse our world with these ancient worlds. For example, when we read the word *marriage,* we need to remember that for ancient Jews such as Abraham and Moses, or even for Jesus and Paul, this word pointed to a social and cultural practice that was very different from our modern American idea of marriage. The discrepancy arises particularly from the completely different social and cultural worldviews that characterize ancient Mediterraneans and modern Americans.

For centuries, Bible readers shared the assumption that the world behind the text and the world of the reader (especially up to the 1800s) were the same. This is illustrated by how medieval artists depicted ancient persons such as Jesus or Mary — dressed in contemporary clothing similar to what the artists wore. Because readers thought they shared the general mental worldview of the biblical authors, they did not think they needed any special procedures for examining the world behind the text.

The danger for us readers today is that, unless we recognize the strangeness of the biblical world, we tend to identify our concerns with theirs and think that our solutions to problems would be just like theirs. Reading for the meaning of an ancient text requires us to bridge the gap between the ancient world and our own.

Scholars try to close this gap by becoming more acutely aware of how the culture of the ancient Jews or that of the early Christians functioned. Scholars have been buoyed by the success of anthropological and social science models to become more aware of the cultural meanings that the original author and audience shared.

In order to appreciate the social and cultural difference between the biblical world and ours today, see Victor H. Matthews and Don C. Benjamin, *Social World of Ancient*

Israel 1250 – 587 B.C.E. (Hendrickson) or John J. Pilch and Bruce J. Malina, *Handbook of Biblical Social Values* (Hendrickson).

The hermeneutic gap

A common problem that produces anxiety for many readers is the conflict of interpretations that occurs when different readers read the same text in different ways. We overcome this gap by developing a clearer understanding of interpretation theory (called hermeneutics). Since we have usually been conditioned to assume that there can be only one meaning for Scripture, we are unsettled when others, especially those within our own faith communities, interpret the Bible differently from us. Since the text is the same, different interpretations must be traced either to the personal differences of the readers or to the different ways of reading the text.

"In the Scriptures, the words are not simple, as some people think. There are very many hidden meanings in them."

— *ST. JEROME*
Commentary on the Vocation of Isaiah

The first source of different interpretations is the differences in readers themselves. Not only do readers have different abilities and reading skills but they also make personal choices about what they want to discover in the text. Some people use the Bible as a source for history, archaeology, psychology, or comparative literature. These different interests and concerns lead the inquirers to highlight certain features of the biblical text rather than others. Problems arise when they confuse their particular interest with what the author intended or assume that what they have discovered is all there is to discover about this particular text.

The second source of conflicting interpretations is based on different theories of interpretation. The most obvious difference is between those who insist that the author's originally intended meaning should guide the interpretation and those who do not. For the former, the historical-critical method becomes the principal method of interpretation. For the latter, the meaning of the text is considered to be plain and clear simply upon reading it.

Because this latter approach seldom acknowledges the significance of the gap between the world behind the text and our own, it considers the historical-critical method unnecessary. These readers find a close connection between what the text says and what it appears to mean. This plain meaning is, however, too often a modern meaning imposed upon the ancient text. The original meaning of the author is confused with whatever meaning is perceived simply by picking up the Bible and reading what its words say. Whatever one understands from the text is assumed to be the divinely inspired meaning. But we must remember that the inspired meaning is the one that the original author intended. Discovering this meaning is very difficult today without using the historical-critical method.

HOW SCRIPTURE SCHOLARS CAN HELP READERS

A CATHOLIC CRITIQUE
OF FUNDAMENTALIST INTERPRETATION

From the Pontifical Biblical Commission's *The Interpretation of the Bible in the Church (1993):*

"Fundamentalist interpretation starts from the principle that the Bible, being the Word of God, inspired and free from error, should be read and interpreted literally in all its details. But by 'literal interpretation' it understands a naively literalist interpretation, one, that is to say, which excludes every effort at understanding the Bible that takes account of its historical origins and development. It is opposed, therefore, to the use of the historical-critical method, as indeed to the use of any other scientific method for the interpretation of Scripture. . . . Fundamentalism is right to insist on the divine inspiration of the Bible, the inerrancy of the Word of God and other biblical truths included in its five fundamental points. But its way of presenting these truths is rooted in an ideology which is not biblical, whatever the proponents of this approach might say. For it demands an unshakable adherence to rigid doctrinal points of view and imposes, as the only source of teaching for Christian life and salvation, a reading of the Bible which rejects all questioning and any kind of critical research."

Here are some of the problems of fundamentalist interpretation:

It refuses to accept the historical character of biblical revelation. It does not admit that the inspired Word of God has been expressed in human language by human authors possessed of limited capacities and resources. Thus, the reader

- treats the biblical text as if it had been dictated word-for-word by the Spirit;

- fails to recognize that the Bible was formulated in language conditioned by various times.

It pays no attention to the literary norms and human ways of thinking in the biblical texts. Many of these norms are the result of a long process covering diverse historical situations.

It unduly stresses the inerrancy of certain details in the biblical texts, especially in what concerns historical events or supposedly scientific truth. Thus, the reader

- often historicizes material that, from the start, never claimed to be historical;
- considers historical everything reported or recounted with verbs in the past tense, failing to take account of the possibility of symbolic or figurative meaning.

It does not consider the development of the gospel tradition. Fundamentalist interpretation naively confuses the final stage (what evangelists wrote) with the initial stage (the words and deeds of Jesus).

It tends to adopt very narrow points of view. Thus, the reader

- accepts the literal reality of an ancient, out-of-date cosmology, simply because it is found in the Bible;
- relies on a noncritical reading of certain texts of the Bible to reinforce political ideas and social attitudes marked by prejudices (such as racism) contrary to the gospel.

Its attachment to the principle "Scripture alone" produces an anti-Church attitude. Thus, the reader

- separates the interpretation of the Bible from tradition;
- fails to realize that the New Testament took form within the Christian Church, whose existence preceded the composition of the texts;

HOW SCRIPTURE SCHOLARS CAN HELP READERS

- gives little importance to the creeds, doctrines, and liturgical practices of the Church tradition, as well as to the Church's teaching function (Magisterium);
- accepts the fundamentalist approach as a form of private interpretation, which does not acknowledge that the Church is founded on the Bible and draws its life and inspiration from Scripture.

Reading the Bible without the historical-critical method is like taking a journey with an out-of-date map. Even if you follow it correctly, you still get lost! As confusion sets in, finding your way becomes more difficult because your map pictures a reality that no longer exists. Errors multiply because your assumptions about the validity of the map are misplaced. If the gap between the biblical writers' worlds and ours is not bridged by the historical-critical method, errors multiply because our assumptions about reading the Bible are no longer appropriate or adequate for guiding our journey today.

If you wish to find out more about these issues of interpretation, see Raymond E. Brown, *Responses to 101 Questions on the Bible* (Paulist Press) or John Barton, *Reading the Old Testament: Method in Biblical Study* (Westminster / John Knox Press).

No Magic Solutions: Only Hard Work Helps

The Bible can be read and interpreted in many ways for many reasons. All of these different readings are necessary to fathom the depths of its meaning and discover its application to our lives. But first we must always pay attention to the meaning that the authors intended. Since this is the meaning inspired by God, we must use every resource we can to understand it.

The Bible is not only God's Word but also the Church's book. There was revelation before the Bible was written, and God's self-revelation to us today is not limited to the pages of the book. The Bible is one special way in which God comes to meet us. What we get out of it will depend on how attentive, careful, and skillful we are at discovering what it contains.

As a book, the biblical revelation must be read and interpreted through our human efforts. It does not work magically, without our effort, nor does it give us all the answers for every problem we face. But it does reveal the God who invites us into a relationship and leads us deeper into that relationship. Our challenge as readers is to bring the Bible to life.

Questions for Reflection and Group Discussion

1. *Describe the three worlds of the text for Lincoln's Gettysburg Address. What difficulties do we have in understanding Lincoln's meaning?*

HOW SCRIPTURE SCHOLARS CAN HELP READERS

2. *Why is the original situation of a communication so important for determining its meaning?*

3. *When we apply the New Testament message to our lives, what problems can emerge if we do not understand the difference between our world and the world of Jesus?*

4. *What does it mean to say that the past is not just prior to us but a different mental and cultural experience? How does this affect our understanding of Jesus and his message?*

5. *Why is there never just one meaning for any biblical text?*

CHAPTER TWELVE

Bringing God's Word to Life

In his second letter to the Christian communities in Corinth, Paul reminds them that "the letter kills, but the Spirit gives life" (2 Corinthians 3:6). This saying reveals the outlook of a predominantly oral culture in which few people could read and all reading was done out loud rather than silently to oneself. Writing was a mystery because the strange markings on the papyrus seemed to solidify spoken words in ink on the page. These words could then remain intact, like an entombed body, and later be brought to life whenever someone read them out loud.

Recall also that in the Hebrew language only consonants were written down, so determining the meaning of a word, phrase, or sentence required supplying the right vowels when reading aloud. As Paul noted, the words on the page were dead until someone breathed life into them by reading. Reading, then, was a process of bringing the words to life.

Our biblical reading journey is such a process. The printed Bible just lies there on our bookshelf or on our nightstand, its words dead and its meanings inanimate until we open it up and vivify them. Reading the Bible is a way of bringing God's Word to life. When we read it, we first bring the words to life by transferring their meaning from the inked page into ideas in our mind.

"What other life can there be without knowledge of the Scriptures, for through these Christ Himself, who is the life of the faithful, becomes known."

— ST. JEROME
Letter 30

We bring God's Word to life in another way when we translate the ideas into action. Our reading is never complete until we bring God's words to our life situation. In step three of the ABC method, we connect the biblical meanings to our life. We bring these meanings to bear on the circumstances of our life and let ourselves, our situations, and our world be changed by what we read. God's Word becomes "living and active" (Hebrews 4:12). Our goal is to bring the Word to life, not merely to study it.

The Emmaus Journey: A Model for Our Bible Pilgrimage

When we bring the biblical word to life both in our minds and in our actions, our journey becomes not just a geographical journey but also a pilgrimage. A pilgrimage is a journey to a sacred place. But the outward, physical journey is accompanied by an inner, spiritual journey to the center of our faith. On a pilgrimage, we reach the sacred destination and simultaneously meet the God whose presence makes the location sacred. So with our Bible journey, we move through the Bible's pages in order to come face-to-face with the God who speaks to us through these words. The final destination of our Bible journey is not a place but a person, not intellectual comprehension but interpersonal community.

In chapter 24 of his Gospel, Luke provides a captivating image of what our biblical journey is like. On the first Easter, two disciples, disappointed because the tomb is empty and Jesus' body is gone, have concluded that their hopes about Jesus were misplaced. So they begin their journey away from Jerusalem toward home.

On the way, they meet a stranger who walks with them. Since Luke tells us that this mysterious stranger is really the risen Jesus, we understand the conversation differently from the way the disciples do. As they walk along discussing the meaning of Scripture, the stranger explains how everything pointed to a messiah who would suffer. The disciples invite the stranger to eat with them, and suddenly "in the breaking of the bread" (Luke 24:35) they recognize the stranger as the risen Jesus. When Christ vanishes, they rush back to Jerusalem to share their good news with the other disciples.

In this wonderful story, Luke provides a model for the journey of our Christian lives. Like these disciples, as we go along our way, Jesus accompanies us even though we don't always recognize him. Through our reading and exploring of the meaning of Scripture, we become aware of God's plan for salvation. We also recognize Christ's presence in our eucharistic meal, and strangers vanish as we all become one in Christ. These disciples are a mirror of us.

Luke also outlines the stages in our Bible reading journey. As the disciples walk with Jesus, their journey moves from stage to stage.

From co-presence to conversation

After the stranger begins to accompany them, he poses a question that redirects their attention and engages them in a new conversation. "What are you discussing?" This invitation to dialogue is eagerly accepted. The disciples launch into a description not only of the facts about the recent events of Jesus' prophetic ministry and death but also about their interpretation or meaning. "We had hoped that he was the one to redeem Israel."

But these hopes have been dashed. The disciples speak of all this in the past tense. Jesus' life is not yet a gospel life but just another life in which the powers of death have triumphed. The news about the empty tomb and the report that Jesus is alive have not yet become "good news." Words about Jesus are no substitute for an experience of him as the risen Christ. Words alone cannot convince them that he is really risen.

From conversation to companionship

At this point the stranger begins a revisionist reading of their Scriptures. Like the Ethiopian, the disciples know the words but not the proper context in which to understand their deeper meaning. Everything they have told the stranger about Jesus is correct, but they lack the essential insight that the promised redeemer would triumph through weakness and suffering instead of through military and miraculous power. So Jesus reinterprets the whole of Scripture in the light of his own suffering.

By now, the day is getting on, and they have been enjoying the conversation so much that they invite the stranger to eat with them. The mysterious stranger is invited to be a companion and share their meal.

From companionship to co-mission

As they sit together celebrating their developing relationship, the stranger "took bread, blessed and broke it, and gave it to them" (Luke 24:30). Finally their eyes are opened. The stranger is the risen Christ. But as soon as they recognize him, he vanishes from their sight. Immediately, they want to share this experience with others. Their companionship is transformed into a co-mission to share their good news with others. They rush back to Jerusalem to tell the other disciples.

From co-mission to community

When they get back, eager to share their good news, they cannot get a word in. The other disciples blurt out first that Jesus has appeared to them. As so many missionaries discover when they eagerly bring the news of God's presence to others, God has already been there! But they do share their own version of the good news. Their mutual sharing forms the community of those who have experienced the risen Christ in their lives. Their common experience of Christ now bonds them into the Christian community.

Bringing the biblical words to life is often aided by sharing what we are discovering. As the story of Philip and the Ethiopian illustrated, difficulties are easier to overcome when we share them instead of struggling with them alone. And a shared journey is nearly always more enjoyable than one we take alone. Finding companions for our biblical journey makes our trip more pleasant. The word *companion* comes from the word that means "share bread with us." For us Christians, the great sharing of bread is our celebration of Eucharist. Just as the Eucharist is our primary model for sharing the Christian life, so its pattern can also be a model for sharing the biblical word with one another.

A Eucharistic Model for Scripture Sharing

As a eucharistic people, our Christian lives are stamped by how Jesus gives himself again and again in the form of bread and wine as nourishment for our lives. The fourfold pattern that characterizes our eucharistic response is rooted in Jesus' own actions: "He took bread, blessed and broke it, and gave it to them" (Luke 24:30).

> "Thanks be to the Gospel, by means of which we also, who did not see Christ when He came into this world, seem to be with Him when we read His deeds."
>
> — *ST. AMBROSE*
> *Concerning Widows, 62*

This dynamic pattern of the Eucharist — take, bless, break, share — also provides the pattern for sharing our biblical journey. These four actions constitute the four steps for our Bible sharing. They guide us to take up the Bible, to bless God and expect a communication for our own lives, to break the biblical books into manageable meanings, and to share our understanding of God's saving message with others.

He took bread

Just as Jesus took the physical bread, so we must take up the Bible. Nothing happens until we do. The meanings remain locked up within its covers, inert and useless for our lives. Food on the supermarket shelves looks great and promises nourishment, but it does nothing for us until we buy it, prepare it, and eat it. The same is true of the Bible.

Although there are many helpful books about the Scriptures, they are no substitute for the real thing. No amount of knowledge about the Bible can substitute for the experience of reading the Bible itself. By reading the Bible we become familiar with God's personality and the ways in which God prefers to relate to us. When we actually read the Scriptures, we do more than read words; we encounter a person. So taking up the Bible is different from taking up any other book.

He blessed

Blessing is a biblical idea that needs some explanation. For the ancients, blessing described God's everyday care for us. Besides the spectacular events through which the people learned that God cared for them — creation, the exodus, the giving of the land, the restoration after the exile — there were the ordinary events that also showed God's loving providence. The everyday experiences of the divine gifts of health, wealth, children, family, friends, good harvests, and all the little things that make our lives satisfactory and enjoyable were recognized as God's blessings.

Through these divine blessings, we live long and happy lives. Since we cannot produce any of these blessings ourselves but must depend on God alone to give them, when we bless we do not cause these blessings but ask God to give them. When Jesus blesses bread, he is asking God to communicate life to us through the bread. This is the spiritual life — God's own life in us — which our material food cannot give.

Just as God communicates life to us through the bread that is Jesus, so God also imparts life to us through the word of the Bible. Whenever we read and reflect upon the meaning of the Bible, we can ask God to empower us to make our everyday lives better. Our Bible reading makes us more familiar with God's favorite ways of entering into everyday situations to bless them. We use the Scriptures to discover clues about God's hidden presence in our midst. Through our reading, our eyes are opened to recognize the blessings God has given and continues to give.

He broke

Bread is no good for nourishment unless it is broken, chewed, digested, and transformed into substances our body can use. Likewise, the bread of God's Word is no good for our spiritual nourishment unless we break it down into meanings that help us to live better Christian lives.

BRINGING GOD'S WORD TO LIFE

The process of breaking a text down into intelligible meanings is interpretation, that is, understanding not only what the text says but also what it means. In step two of our ABC method, when we move beyond the simple reading of the words of the Bible "to understand what God has wished to communicate to us, [we] must carefully investigate what meaning the biblical writers actually had in mind; that will also be what God chose to manifest through their words" (Vatican II, *On Revelation* no. 12).

After we discover what the Bible meant to its original audience, we can then determine what it means for us today. We study the Bible because we believe that God's revealed Word communicates a message that still applies today. God is always working in our world to transform it into the world God wants it to be. Through reading and interpreting the Bible, we detect God's presence and discover God's vision for a transformed world.

He shared

We humans are not the only animals that eat, but we are the only ones who cook! And much of our cooking is not merely for sustenance but for showing others that we care. Food always means more to us than biological nourishment. It communicates many symbolic meanings that reveal our social values.

Eating alone is not much fun. Sharing food signifies our willingness to share our lives. So we tend to be very selective

MAKING YOUR JOURNEY

about the people we dine with. We share bread with the people we want to share our lives. Jesus' inclusive dining was a sign of his universal love. Just as Christ was willing to share himself with anyone who wanted or needed his company, so we Christians must learn to share ourselves with others.

The word of the Bible, like the bread that is Jesus, is for everyone. Our discovery of God through the Bible is an experience we are expected to share with others. Meanings cannot exist in isolation. Meaning is shared when we speak it. Speaking expresses (pushes out!) our inner experience in the shared realm of public language. Others now hear our words and are expected to respond. So dialogue begins.

Using the Model for Small-Group Sharing

The four steps in the eucharistic process provide a model for the practice of small-group Bible sharing. As the group gathers in a circle, the Bible is reverently placed in the center of the group. A candle is lighted to remind us that Christ our light is present to guide our path through Scripture.

One of the group members then **takes** the book and slowly reads the passage chosen for prayer and discussion. At the end of the reading, after time for reflection, one member prays for God to **bless** the group with the presence and guidance of the Holy Spirit to open their minds and hearts to hear, heed, and apply God's message to their lives.

BRINGING GOD'S WORD TO LIFE

After a time of prayerful reflection in silence, the group begins to **break** the passage into its meanings. After rereading the passage, they consider what the author said and what the passage meant to its first readers. This can be done simply by considering who said what, to whom, in what situation, in what way, and for what reasons. Then they consider what this text means now as they make connections between it and their lives during the coming week.

Then they **share** these reflections with one another. After this conversation, the group session ends with a song, a prayer, and the commissioning of the members to share this message with their family, friends, business associates, and anyone with whom they will come into contact during the coming week.

In this way, the Word of God is just like the bread and wine of the Eucharist. When we take, bless, break, and share the Bible, we are simultaneously taken, blessed, broken, and shared by God's mysterious and loving presence. We are taken into the community of brothers and sisters who are identified as Christians because we are formed in the image of Jesus. His story becomes our story; his example becomes our guide for living; his vision and values become our guidelines for consecrating and reordering the world.

> "If on any day there is no instruction [in the Christian gathering], let each one at home take the Scriptures and read sufficiently in passages that they find profitable."
>
> — *HIPPOLYTUS*
> *Apostolic Traditions,* 36

Your Bible Journey

As you end this book and prepare to embark on your Bible journey, the Emmaus journey illustrates what awaits you. When you begin, you invite the mysterious presence of God to accompany you. The words of the Bible begin a conversation. As you read God's words, you begin to realize that all that you thought was so clear, especially your presuppositions about God and God's plan, need to be revised in the light of your discovery of new meanings. Your dialogue with the text, both through the questions you ask it and the even more challenging questions it asks you, gradually transforms you. As you journey with the Bible, it subtly refocuses your attention and redescribes your understanding of the events of your world and their meaning in relation to Christ.

As your relationship grows on your journey, you move from conversation to companionship and sharing in the eucharistic meal. You imitate the eucharistic actions of Jesus, discovering him present once again in the bread and wine that you share at communion time. As with the Emmaus

BRINGING GOD'S WORD TO LIFE

disciples, this meal is the culminating moment when you recognize him "in the breaking of the bread" (Luke 24:35).

But companionship and meal sharing are never the final experience. We also call the Eucharist the Mass, which comes from the Latin words of dismissal — *Ita, Missa* est (Go, you are sent forth). We gather together to be nourished in order to take up our mission. We continue in our lives the task of sharing the good news of Jesus' rising to new life. Your companionship gives way to co-mission, and this leads to the creation and maintenance of the Christian community that gathers to celebrate God's mysterious transforming presence in word and sacrament.

As a seeker, then, enjoy your journey with the mysterious stranger who already walks with you. Discover God the same way that these Emmaus seekers did. Be attentive to the moments when words you thought you knew so well break open to reveal unsuspected surprises.

Just as Jesus was recognized on the Emmaus journey when questions turned into conversation, when conversation sparked companionship, and when recognition of a mysterious companion kindled evangelization, so will he again be recognized this way on your Bible reading journey. And my fondest hope for you is that you will be able to say, like those Emmaus pilgrims when their journey was done, "Were not our hearts burning within us while he was talking to us on the road, while he was opening the scriptures to us?" (Luke 24:32).

MAKING YOUR JOURNEY

Glossary

apocalyptic. (Greek: to reveal) A modern, scholarly label for Jewish and Christian writing that emphasizes God's imminent intervention into our history to transform it.

Apocrypha. (Greek: hidden things) An ancient Jewish or Christian book that is not included in the biblical canon (also called noncanonical). Such writings can be described as apocryphal.

Aramaic. The Semitic language related to Hebrew, widely used after about 300 B.C., which was spoken by Jesus and the apostle Paul.

canon. (Greek: a measuring ruler) The official list of books that belong to the biblical collection. Such books are called canonical.

captivity epistles. Four Pauline letters (Philippians, Colossians, Ephesians and Philemon) that are believed to have been written from prison.

catholic epistles. A traditional designation for James, Jude, 1 and 2 Peter, 1, 2, and 3 John that recognizes their importance for the whole ("catholic") Church.

codex. An ancient manuscript in leaf or book form that was sewn together at the fold instead of rolled as a scroll.

criticism. (Greek: judgment) A general term for the scholarly study of the Bible. It includes scientific, historical, and literary methods plus various approaches for discovering the meanings of the text.

Dead Sea Scrolls. A group of manuscripts found in 1947 in caves along the Dead Sea. They include Old Testament books and commentaries and other books that were probably part of the library of the Essene community. These Jewish sectarians lived at Qumran, which was destroyed by the Romans in A.D. 68.

deuterocanonical. (Greek: second canon) Seven books (Wisdom, Sirach, Baruch, 1 and 2 Maccabees, Tobit, and Judith) and parts of two others (Esther and Daniel) that are not in the Hebrew canon but were in the Greek Septuagint. They are considered canonical by Catholics and noncanonical (apocryphal) by Protestants.

epistle. A letter generally written for public reading in the Christian assembly to proclaim the Christian message, to teach and explain doctrine, and to identify and encourage proper Christian behavior.

exegesis. (Greek: draw out, hence, explanation or interpretation) The explanation of the meaning of the biblical text, in particular through the use of the historical-critical method, to understand the author's intended meaning.

form criticism. The scholarly study of the origin and transmission of the biblical texts and of the sources used in their composition.

fundamentalism. When used to designate an approach to biblical interpretation, this term normally identifies a precritical approach that does not employ the historical-critical method and that separates the Bible from its location in the Christian tradition. The result is a naively literalist reading of the Bible to support rigidly conservative doctrines.

Gnosticism. (Greek: knowledge) A form of religion that stressed that salvation and the right relationship with God come through esoteric or mystical knowledge. It was rejected by Christianity in the second century as heretical. In 1945–46 a library of some fifty Gnostic texts was discovered at Nag Hammadi in Egypt.

gospel. (Greek: evangelion; Anglo-Saxon: Godspell or good news) A general description of the Christian message. Later it became primarily associated with the four written narrative presentations of this message according to Mark, Matthew, Luke, and John.

Hebrew. The Semitic language used by the Israelites from the fourteenth to the fifth century B.C., after which it was retained in the sacred written texts but was gradually replaced in everyday life by Aramaic and then Greek for Jews in the diaspora.

Hellenization. (Greek: Hellas, or Greece) The domination by Greek language, culture, and thought of the whole Mediterranean world as a result of the conquests of Alexander the Great in 333–323 B.C.

hermeneutics. (Greek: interpretation) The scholarly study of the theory and practice of textual interpretation.

historical criticism. A general term for modern critical, biblical scholarship that attempts to situate ancient texts in their historical circumstances in order to discover the original meaning intended by the authors.

inerrancy. In the theological sense, inerrancy means that the biblical books are without error when properly interpreted and understood. The Catholic interpretation of this doctrine limits the inerrancy to the divinely revealed mysteries and the "truth which God wanted to put into the sacred writings for the sake of our salvation" (*Dei Verbum*, #11). Any errors of historical or scientific fact are attributed to the limitations of the human authors.

inspiration. In the theological sense, inspiration refers to God's assistance of human authors in the composition of the biblical books so that the divinely revealed message was communicated through their human words. "Inspiration" does not describe *how* God worked through human authors.

Koine. (Greek: common) The Greek language of daily conversation and writing used throughout the Mediterranean world following the conquests of Alexander the Great. All of our New Testament texts were written in this dialect.

literal sense. The meaning that the author intended at the time of writing and that the written words expressed. Determining this meaning is the goal of the historical-critical method of Scripture scholarship. For Scripture scholars, to "take things literally" means to determine what the original author meant.

Masoretic Text. (MT) The definitive text of the Hebrew Bible, with vowels (indicated by dots or points) and punctuation supplied by Jewish grammarians (the Masoretes) from the seventh to tenth centuries A.D.

method. (Greek: a way over) A general and repeatable set of scientific procedures used in order to explain texts. The historical-critical method combines historical and literary procedures to determine the original situation and the author's intended meaning.

mystery. A spiritual reality that transcends human knowledge and thus can never be comprehended fully.

New Testament. The official collection of twenty-seven sacred Christian texts that are considered revealed, inspired, inerrant regarding the truths of salvation, and authoritative for Christian belief and practice.

Old Testament. The collection of sacred texts from the Jewish tradition that have been adopted by Christians. The number of books varies from thirty-nine (Protestant) to forty-six (Catholic) because of the inclusion of books written in Greek for Hellenistic Jews, which were included in the ancient Septuagint translation. (See **deuterocanonical.**)

palimpsest. (Greek: rub again) A parchment manuscript that has been erased (by scraping) and written on again.

parallelism. A distinctive formal characteristic of Hebrew poetry in which balanced couplets generally relate to each other either through repetition, which reinforces similarity (synonymous) or through contrast, which expresses difference (antithetic). Hebrew poets also used a variety of other variations.

pastoral epistles. A convenient description of the Pauline letters 1 and 2 Timothy and Titus, which incorporate the "pastoral" advice of Paul to these helpers. Scholars are divided about whether these were written by Paul or perhaps by a later follower of his tradition.

Pentateuch. (Greek: five scrolls) The first five books of the Old Testament, also called the Law (Torah) of Moses.

pericope. (Greek: to cut around) A short section or passage of writing, such as a small division or unit of Scripture taken for reading or analysis.

prophetic literature. The collection of writings by people God called to speak God's message to the Israelites and their rulers. The prophets' intent was not to foretell the future but to recognize God's presence in current events and to identify the consequences of people's disregarding or neglecting this presence.

proverb. A short memorable saying that incorporates the traditional wisdom gained from careful observation of nature and human life. A proverb is usually expressed in poetic parallel form for greater impact and easier recall.

psalm. (Greek: songs) A song accompanied by music. The biblical book of Psalms consists of 150 psalms divided into five parts. These songs express the whole spectrum of human response to God.

pseudepigrapha. (Greek: falsely entitled) Works written in the name of another (usually more famous) person or attributed to another as author. Scholars also use it to designate the collection of works that are apocryphal.

redaction criticism. The scholarly analysis of the composition of texts to discover how sources were used in the process of editing (redacting). This type of study is used in particular to carefully analyze the editorial process of the synoptic Gospels to illuminate the unique form, content, and function of each and to appreciate each author's artistry.

revelation. (Latin: to unveil) The free self-disclosure of God's person and plan for human salvation.

GLOSSARY

rhetorical criticism. The scholarly analysis of texts in order to understand their persuasive function, in particular how they have been shaped to accomplish their effects on the audience.

Septuagint. (LXX) (Latin: seventy) A Greek translation of the Hebrew Bible done in Egypt beginning about 250 B.C. It also included several books written in Greek. It was adopted by early Greek-speaking Christians as their Bible.

source criticism. The scholarly identification and analysis of the different sources that were used to shape a text, such as the documentary hypothesis of four sources of the Pentateuch (JEDP) or the two sources (Mark and Q) for resolving the synoptic problem.

synoptic Gospels. (Greek: seen with one glance) The gospels of Matthew, Mark, and Luke; because of their literary interrelationships and their generally similar structure, they can be put into parallel columns for closer examination.

TaNaKh. (TNK) The modern Jewish, scholarly name for the Hebrew Bible derived from the initial letters for the three divisions of the Bible: Torah (Law), Nevi'im (Prophets), and Ketuvim (Writings).

textual criticism. The scholarly study of ancient manuscripts to ascertain the original form of the text and to trace the history of its transmission through variant forms.

typology. A style of biblical interpretation in which Old Testament persons or events are understood as patterns or models for New Testament persons or events.

Vulgate. (Latin: crowd, thus, common) The Latin translation of the Bible by Jerome, translated from the original Hebrew and Greek near the end of the fourth century A.D.

wisdom literature. The collection of traditional learning that deals with the mystery of our world and of everyday life. The Jewish tradition sought to merge this secular tradition with their specifically religious beliefs and guidelines (Torah).

For further reading, Loyola Press also offers a Scripture study series, *Catholic Perspectives: Six Weeks with the Bible.* Created for busy people, this practical series helps Catholics learn about Scripture while deepening their relationship with God. Each six-week discovery guide focuses on a specific book in the Bible, then explains Scripture and applies it to everyday life. The guides are faithful to Church teachings and the best biblical scholarship, and they include thought-provoking questions for group discussion or personal reflection. This innovative series is appealing to beginners as well as to those already familiar with the Bible. For more information, please call (800) 621-1008.